U.S. Presidents:
Past and Present

BY
GEORGE R. LEE

Mark Twain Media, Inc., Publishers
Distributed by Carson-Dellosa Publishing LLC

Visit us at www.carsondellosa.com

HPS 221297

Table of Contents

Introduction: The Making of a President

This is a book about the presidents of the United States. Who will be chosen in future elections is not clear; we will just have to wait and see. The fact that we have had no women, Asian, or Latino presidents in the past does not mean it will never happen. It means only that in the past, they have never been considered for the office. In fact, in the 2008 campaign, an African-American was elected president for the first time, there was a female candidate for vice president, and another woman was a strong contender for the Democratic presidential nomination.

The Constitution requires that the president be chosen by the Electoral College. In the early days, the electors were chosen by state legislatures, but by the 1830s the people were choosing the electors. The number of electors a state has is equal to the number of members it is entitled to in the House of Representatives and Senate. Every state has two senators, but the number in the House is based on population. A state with five House members has seven electors (5 + 2), while a state with 20 House members has 22 electors (20 + 2). This has often affected who will be chosen as a presidential candidate. Candidates from states with large numbers of electoral votes have a better chance of being chosen than those from states with small populations.

The Constitution itself offers few obstacles to becoming president. It requires only that the person be at least 35 years old, born in the United States or of U.S. citizens, and have spent fourteen years in the United States. If those were the only criteria, over 70 million Americans would be eligible to become president. But obviously there are more hurdles that separate a person from the office.

A candidate must be nominated by a political party. George Washington was the only exception. The parties began to form in the 1790s, and while the party labels have changed over the years, the role of political parties has not. The political parties are groups that form around a leader or a common cause. They first developed from the debate over the Constitution; those favoring it were called Federalists and those opposing it were called Anti-Federalists. When the national government was formed, the debates between followers of Alexander Hamilton and Thomas Jefferson led to the forming of the Federalist and Republican Parties (not the present Republicans, however). In time, the Federalists died out, and everyone was Republican.

Rival candidates divided the Republicans in 1824 with the followers of John Quincy Adams becoming the National Republicans and those of Andrew Jackson the Democratic-Republicans. After Jackson won the presidency in 1828, his opponents formed the Whig Party, which was later replaced by the Republican Party. Besides the major parties, we have had a number of "third" parties that have come along, and in some cases, these parties have affected the national election. In 1912, the third party candidate, Theodore Roosevelt, received more votes than the Republican candidate, William H. Taft.

To win the party nomination is very important, but what does it take to do that? A person must have ambition and want the job badly enough to work hard to get it. The campaign process is a torture test of developing policy statements, giving speeches, shaking hands, organizing, raising money, and avoiding costly mistakes. A candidate chosen in the twenty-first century will probably spend at least two years of hard work to get nominated. The candidate has to believe in himself or herself, as well as the policies he or she wants to carry out when they get elected.

The candidate must also be <u>intelligent</u>. He or she must take a position on a wide variety of topics and then defend his or her decisions on foreign and domestic policies. In the past, some candidates were able to get by with vague statements about where they stood on issues, but it is unlikely that anyone will be able to do that in the future.

<u>Personality</u> certainly makes a difference. A person who is charming, witty, is careful about controlling his or her temper, and chooses words well is going to draw media attention and adoring supporters. The role of personality has become more important in the age of television.

<u>Appearance</u> is important. The candidate must look like a leader and act like one. Image is important to success in seeking high office.

The candidate must be able to <u>draw support from a wide variety of backers</u>. The candidate has to be appealing to senior citizens, working moms, the rich, the poor, the middle class, and people from a wide variety of religious, racial, and ethnic backgrounds in order to win. The candidate does not have to please everyone, but he or she has to please enough people to get the support needed for a strong campaign.

The candidate has to have <u>good advisors</u> to help guide him or her in weak areas. A person growing up in New York City may understand city issues but have no knowledge of agricultural issues. He or she may have been a governor and understand how an executive branch works, but be weak in foreign policy. A senator may have experience with the legislative branch and maybe even foreign policy, but he or she will need guidance in administration. Getting the right advice is critical to running for office successfully.

<u>Being decisive</u> is also important. If the candidate cannot make a firm decision and stick to it, the public will wonder if he or she is capable of being a strong leader for the nation. On the other hand, sticking to a policy that draws too much opposition is foolhardy. The candidate has to know when to compromise and when to stand firm.

The same qualities that make a good candidate make a person successful as president: ambition, intelligence, personality, appearance, keeping public support, choosing good advisors, and being decisive. It also helps to have a family that does not embarrass, a spouse who can turn on the charm, and a good economic situation and world peace during his or her term of office.

This book is about those who have served as president. It will try to describe the individual's background and his successes and failures in the highest office in our land. As future voters of the United States, you will be choosing future presidents. Study the candidates, decide for yourself what qualities you like and dislike in each of them, and choose which will make the nation stronger and better.

Why Might a Person Want to Be President?

Every four years, a number of leaders announce that they want to be their party's nominee for president of the United States. Why do they do it? Below are some reasons for their interest in the job.

1. The person feels he or she is the best qualified person to be president. He or she has had experience in government that makes him or her outstanding. He or she has been governor of a state, an important member of Congress, or a member of the cabinet.

2. The person is attracted by the power of the office. The president is unique. He or she will be the spokesperson for the nation. The president will choose the cabinet and other high officials. Everywhere the president goes, large crowds come out to greet him or her, and the press records his or her every word. Theodore Roosevelt called the presidency "a bully pulpit." When the president speaks, the world listens.

3. The candidate has an agenda he or she wants made into law. He or she often doesn't like the way the nation is going and wants it to change direction. This is often true when the current president is of the opposite party as the candidate.

4. He or she doesn't like the other candidates and enters the race to stop them. If the other would-be seekers of the party nomination are conservative, a party liberal may run in protest.

5. Many who run are encouraged by friends and admirers to take the big step to the top. Sometimes this urging is unrealistic, and the candidate finds that his or her own desire is not shared by most other Americans.

6. He or she will have a place in history. His or her name will be on that list of famous people along with Washington, Jefferson, and the Roosevelts. Other political leaders are forgotten a few years after they leave office, but presidents will be included in encyclopedias and other reference materials for centuries.

7. There are many perks that go with the job. The salary is good. There are free living accommodations and a staff that is trained to meet your every whim. When you travel, streets are blocked. When you fly, you have a beautiful airplane ready to go. When you go to the ballgame, you have a box seat. You never have to wait your turn at the golf course. You can watch the latest movies at the White House. When you sit at a table, you are the focus of attention.

    You travel around the world on Air Force One and meet great leaders. You invite celebrities to the White House, and they come. The best hotels and restaurants are pleased to have you as a guest, and someone else pays the bills. You can vacation at Camp David or anywhere you want to go.

    When you retire, you will have an excellent pension, Secret Service protection, free medical care, and the opportunity to make money by giving speeches or writing books. Your funeral will be attended by high officials from all over the world, and flags will fly at half-mast.

Why Might a Person *NOT* Want to Be President?

Just as there are many reasons why people want to become the president of the United States, there are also reasons why qualified individuals choose not to run for the office.

1. There is too much sacrifice in getting the job. Running for president is as much fun as running a 50-mile race over all kinds of hurdles. Many will not do it when they think about the weeks of work, loss of privacy, and the hardship on their families.

    There is also a real possibility that he or she will not win. A senator may be idolized in his or her home state, but no one has heard of him or her a few states away. A candidate has to give many speeches, shake thousands of hands, and face endless questions in news conferences.

2. It is very costly to run, and the candidate has to raise millions of dollars. People will invest in the campaign only if they think the candidate has the potential of winning. Many candidates quickly tire of the dinners and fund-raising events.

3. Presidents lose all privacy. Whatever they do, good or bad, important or unimportant, is in the news. When President Ford stumbled a few times, he was ridiculed by stand-up comedians. The president's children are ambushed by photographers from behind trees. Nothing you have ever done is off-limits to the press. They will interview everyone you have ever known.

4. The job is very complicated. John Kennedy said the president never gets to make the easy decisions; he has only the hardest ones. There are people to appoint to the White House staff, executive departments, and independent agencies. There are economic, political, and international issues where everyone has an opinion, and none of your experts agree. There are times when the only choice is between a bad alternative and a terrible alternative.

    Besides national affairs, state and local problems sometimes have to be dealt with by the president. Presidents Kennedy and Lyndon Johnson, for instance, had to pressure southern states to end segregation policies.

    International affairs often cause presidential headaches. Some parts of the world are always danger points: the Middle East, the Balkans, and Asia, among others. The danger of terrorist attacks and biological or nuclear war is real. So many meetings are held on these types of topics that many presidents get little rest when a crisis occurs.

5. The job is dangerous. Four presidents have been killed by assassins (Lincoln, Garfield, McKinley, and Kennedy). Attempts have been made on the lives of others. The president today is well protected by Secret Service agents, but the president is often out in public and is a potential target for anyone wanting instant notoriety.

6. There is a let-down that comes toward the end of the term. Congress is more interested in what the next president will do than what the outgoing president wants done. Once out of office, the ex-president's opinion means little, and most of the time no one cares what he thinks. Once out of office, many presidents have had a difficult time in adjusting to a civilian life.

Name: _____ Date: _____

Campaign Activity

This is a story of a presidential campaign. Candidates A and B have been chosen by their parties, and you are uncertain how to vote. As the campaign continues, decide how you would vote at that moment if the election were held that day. If you are uncertain, put a ? on the line.

_____ 1. The X Party selects "A" as its candidate. "A" is a charming person, but questions have been raised about his or her race for governor a few years ago. However, you certainly like his or her choice of running mate.

_____ 2. The Z Party selects "B" as its candidate. "B" has had experience in state government and has been a U.S. secretary of state. "B" seems more intelligent than "A." "B's" choice for vice president is a person you know little about, and you see no reason to like or dislike him or her.

_____ 3. An issue important to you comes up, and you like "B's" position better than "A's."

_____ 4. The media focuses on "B's" brother-in-law, who is sent to prison for tax evasion.

_____ 5. "A's" advertising campaign portrays "A" as a product of a good, clean, wholesome, average American family. "B's" campaign reveals that "A's" family has been troubled by drug and alcohol abuse.

_____ 6. "B" came from a rich family and attended an elite college. "A's" family was poor, and "A" had to work his or her way through an average college. "A" got very high grades, but "B's" grades were not outstanding.

_____ 7. "A" begins to have heart problems and has to be taken to the emergency room. "B" sends flowers.

_____ 8. "B's" brother dies, but "B" does not go to the funeral. He goes to two key campaign appearances instead.

_____ 9. In a debate, "A" uses figures to make a point that are shown to be incorrect by "B."

_____ 10. The campaign turns nasty. The X Party says that "B" cheated on a college exam, and the Z Party tells about an illegal campaign contribution by a gangster to the "A" campaign.

It is now election day. Which way will you vote? Why?   _____ A or B?

Reasons _____

_____

Are you certain you have made the right choice?   _____ Yes   _____ No

GEORGE WASHINGTON
(1732–1799, P. 1789–1797).

When the electors cast their ballots in 1789, they unanimously chose George Washington for president. He was already a legend and was determined not to let his reputation be tarnished. He was the most famous American of his time and was noted for his courage and character. The old saying goes: "As the twig is bent, so the tree is inclined." He intended for his "tree," the presidency, to stand straight, tall, and proud.

Washington was the son of Augustus and Mary. His father was often away taking care of his iron ore business, so young George was with his mother most of the time. Mary was a very insecure woman; her parents had died when she was 13 years old and had left her with a small fortune. She had always been frugal with money, and she complained about being poor. Augustus was much more generous with the children born to his first marriage than to Mary and her children, which also disturbed her.

Little schooling was available in the area, and George Washington had only seven or eight years in classrooms. He was best at mathematics, but he studied other subjects too. He kept a diary and wrote out rules to live by. He learned the social skills required of a person in the upper class. There were strict rules of courtesy to learn and skills to master. Perhaps the part he enjoyed most was dancing. Much of his time was spent outdoors working, hunting, and fishing. He loved riding horses and exploring the woods. When he was 11 years old, his father died, and more responsibility fell to him as the oldest son of his mother. Running a plantation was hard work, and he became an excellent farmer.

George's half-brother, Lawrence, was his hero. Lawrence had been a militia captain, and he taught George about military subjects. Lawrence named his home Mount Vernon, in honor of a British naval hero. George wanted to join the navy, but his mother refused to give permission. He became a surveyor at the age of 16, a job that gave him the opportunity to buy land on the frontier with very little money. In 1751, he went with Lawrence to the British West Indies, where George contracted smallpox. After he recovered, he returned to Virginia. His brother died in 1752 of tuberculosis, and after the death of Lawrence's wife and daughter, George inherited the plantation at Mount Vernon.

By the time he was a young man, George was 6 feet 2 inches tall, very strong, and a great horseman. He wore size 13 shoes and had gray-blue eyes and brown hair. He kept very careful records of everything; he even calculated that there were 71,000 seeds in a pound of red clover.

In 1753, Washington was made a major in the Virginia militia. He started studying books on military affairs and tactics. In October, the governor sent Major Washington to the forks of the Ohio River where the French were building Fort Duquesne (at Pittsburgh). It was a very rough trip through wilderness. The French refused to stop building the fort, and Washington and his companions returned through heavy snow and bitterly cold weather to give their report. The governor sent him to build a fort and promoted him to lieutenant-colonel. When the French attacked his "Fort Necessity," Washington wrote: "I heard the bullets whistle, and believe me there is something charming in the sound." His poorly-trained men were surrounded and forced to surrender.

In the French and Indian War that followed, Washington went with the British General Braddock's expedition, and he saw British regulars break and run. Washington left the army angry at the way he had been treated as merely a militia officer. He was later assigned the job of protecting Virginia's frontier. Most of his troops were a ragged collection of men, but they successfully held off attacks. His experience with these types of men was important later in his life.

He married Martha Custis in 1759; she was a widow with two children and a large estate. He then served in the colonial legislature. There he learned how difficult it was to get bills passed. He also met many future leaders like Patrick Henry and Thomas Jefferson. He watched as the colonies and England drifted toward war. He dreaded a war, but when the need for independence became more clear to him, he was ready.

In 1775, Congress chose him to lead its army. He refused to take a salary, and Congress only paid for his expenses. "These are times that try men's souls," Thomas Paine wrote, and certainly that was true for Washington. Defeated in battle many times, he refused to quit. He suffered through cold winters with his men, saw men desert, and complained to Congress about their need for shoes and blankets. It has been said that Washington was at his best when conditions were at their worst. He never considered giving up. He would rather have died than surrendered. His efforts paid off at Yorktown, Virginia, with a major victory. Great Britain finally gave the United States its independence.

Washington returned to Mount Vernon, expecting to spend the rest of his life as a farmer. However, he left retirement again when the Constitutional Convention was held in 1787. He was elected president of the Convention, and then he was chosen president of the United States in 1789. It was a job he did not want or ask for, but he put public interest before personal desire.

WASHINGTON AS PRESIDENT. Washington faced five important problems. Problem 1 was organizing the executive branch; he did that by choosing a cabinet. At the time it had only three members: the secretary of state, secretary of the treasury, and secretary of war.

Problem 2 was putting the government on a sound financial basis. That was done by the policies of Secretary of the Treasury Alexander Hamilton. The Bank of the United States was created to handle government funds. When frontier farmers protested against the Whiskey Tax, Washington sent an army to enforce it. When the farmers surrendered, he pardoned them.

Problem 3 was getting the British to leave forts in the West, which was finally accomplished by the Jay Treaty. When wars broke out in Europe between Great Britain and France, Washington stayed neutral. The country was not yet strong enough to get involved in world affairs, and he was able to stay neutral, despite the general opinion that we should help France.

Problem 4 was Indian troubles on the frontier. Three expeditions were sent to fight Indians. The first two ended in humiliating disasters. The third was led by General Anthony Wayne, and the Indians were defeated at Fallen Timbers.

Problem 5 was to create an image for the United States. Remember, at that time we were a very small nation with a weak army and navy. The president was always dignified, holding fancy levees (receptions) and dinners. He said: "There is a rank due to the United States among nations which will be withheld, if not absolutely lost, by the reputation of weakness." He gave every appearance that the United States was in strong hands.

Many issues came up where Washington had to take an unpopular stand, but he always made difficult decisions without concern for personal glory. He knew as much about war and foreign affairs as anyone, so he kept a close eye on the War and State Departments. Economic affairs were more difficult for him to understand, so he gave the secretary of the treasury more freedom to make decisions in that area. He expected honesty and integrity from everyone in government, and would accept nothing less.

Washington was often attacked by writers, and like every president since, he was angry with the press at times. While he was usually able to hold his temper, these attacks sometimes aroused his wrath. One newspaper said he secretly wanted to be a king. At a cabinet meeting, Washington exploded that he would rather be back at Mount Vernon than to be emperor of the world. These attacks no doubt affected his decision not to run for a third term. He voluntarily did what few people with great power had ever done before; he gladly gave up power for a quiet life with his family.

After eight years as president, and despite many pleas that he serve another term, he retired and gladly returned to his plantation at Mount Vernon. His main activity now was raising crops and supervising his workers.

When Washington died in 1799, the nation mourned its loss. He was praised by Richard Henry Lee as being "First in war, first in peace, and first in the hearts of his countrymen." He had performed well every job he had been given and had fearlessly done what he thought was in the best interests of his people.

Washington has been honored by the nation in many ways. He is the only president to have a state named after him, and the nation's capital bears his name. The Washington Monument is by far the tallest structure in the District of Columbia. His face appears on the quarter and the $1 bill. Many counties, cities, schools, and streets bear his name.

Name: _____ Date: _____

Points to Ponder (Washington)

1. Name three qualities Washington had that caused others to admire him so much.

   _____

   _____

2. Name four things that happened during his younger days that helped him when he became a general and the first president.

   _____

   _____

   _____

3. Washington had less education than Jefferson, Madison, Hamilton, and other leaders. Why did they all respect him so much?

   _____

   _____

4. Washington is not as popular now as he was a century ago. Why do you think that is?

   _____

   _____

5. What qualities might a general have that would be helpful as president?

   _____

   _____

   What qualities might a general have that would hurt him as president?

   _____

   _____

 **Explore History**

1. Draw a picture or construct a model of a fort.

2. Make a time line of Washington's military and political career.

3. Research Washington's home, Mount Vernon. Design a travel brochure, including pictures, describing both his home and the area. Convince people to visit.

4. Pretend you were a soldier serving under Washington. Describe his qualities as a good leader. Tell about some of the hardships you endured, especially in the winter.

JOHN ADAMS
(1735–1826, P. 1797–1801)

Washington, D.C., was a city in name only when John Adams moved into the Executive Mansion in 1800. There were tree stumps where roads were to be built and a swamp down by the Potomac River.

Adams was born in Braintree (now Quincy), Massachusetts, in 1735. His family was of old Puritan stock and had come to America around 1640. Young Adams worked on the family farm and studied in the village school. He graduated from Harvard College in 1755, became a teacher while he studied law, and became a lawyer in 1758.

Adams married Abigail in 1764. She was an intelligent woman who was poorly educated, but she became a good reader and a writer of interesting letters. Adams opposed the Stamp Act in 1765 on the basis the colonies were not represented in Parliament. In 1768, he moved to Boston, where his cousin, Sam Adams, was stirring up the people against the British in creative ways. John and Sam did not always think alike, however. When British soldiers were tried for the Boston Massacre, John defended them in court.

Adams was a member of the Continental Congress, and he strongly argued for independence. He was a member of the committee appointed to write a Declaration of Independence; Jefferson wrote the famous document, but Adams defended it when Congress debated it. He served in France and Holland as a diplomat during the Revolution. At the end of the Revolution, he was sent to Paris to negotiate peace terms with Great Britain. In 1785, he was appointed as American ambassador to Great Britain.

In 1789, Adams was chosen as vice president by the electors. He called the vice presidency "the most insignificant office that ever the invention of man contrived or his imagination conceived."

In 1796, Adams was elected president, and Thomas Jefferson was elected vice president. The two men were no longer friends. Jefferson suspected that Adams favored monarchy and disliked him personally. Adams was a hard person to like; he was vain, opinionated, bad-tempered, and stubborn.

ADAMS AS PRESIDENT. When the United States and France were close to fighting a war in 1798, Federalists in Congress passed the Alien and Sedition Acts, making it a crime for anyone to criticize the president or Congress. There was a storm of protest against the new laws; Jefferson and John Madison secretly wrote resolutions passed by the Kentucky and Virginia legislatures attacking the Sedition Act as a violation of the First Amendment. The laws were clearly a legal and political blunder. The possible war with France cleared when Adams defied Federalist opinion and sent a delegation to France to settle differences. He had lost Republican support over the Sedition Act, and then he lost Federalist support.

When Jefferson was elected to replace him, Adams refused to stay for the inauguration. He left office a lonely and bitter man. However, in his old age, he renewed his friendship with Jefferson. As he lay dying on July 4, 1826, 50 years to the day after the Declaration of Independence, his last words were "Thomas Jefferson still survives." He did not know that Jefferson had died that same morning.

Name: _____ Date: _____

Points to Ponder (J. Adams)

1. John Adams acquired many enemies along the way to the presidency. How would you account for a person with his personality becoming president?

    _____

    _____

    _____

2. Washington had been tall and well-built, while Adams was short and round. Do physical appearances have any effect on a president's success? Why?

    _____

    _____

3. The Federalist Party split between Adams and Hamilton supporters. How would that affect the success of any president?

    _____

    _____

    _____

4. Adams was proud of his avoiding war with France. Should we honor those presidents who have succeeded in preventing a war more than we do now?

    _____

    _____

5. Read the First Amendment to the Constitution. What part of that amendment did the Sedition Act probably violate?

    _____

☆ ☆ ☆ **Explore History** ☆ ☆ ☆

1. One of Adams' most important appointments was John Marshall, whom he named as Chief Justice. Why is the choice of justices on the Supreme Court important? Make a time line of John Marshall's career, or write a short biography of his life.

2. Adams called the vice presidency, "the most insignificant office that ever the invention of man contrived or his imagination conceived." What are the duties of the vice president? Make a chart or poster listing presidents that were formerly vice presidents. Include how they became president: through presidential assassination or death, impeachment, and so on.

THOMAS JEFFERSON
(1743–1826, P. 1801–1809)

JULY 4, 1776
When in the
Course of human events,

The British ambassador went to the Executive Mansion one morning and met the president, who was dressed in a dressing gown and slippers. Thomas Jefferson was the first president to be casual in what he wore, but beneath that "Republican simplicity" as he called it, he was one of the most complex men to ever become president.

Thomas was the son of Peter and Jane Jefferson. His father was a self-made man and an important local official. His mother came from a very wealthy family. As a boy, Thomas fished and hunted with his father, who also taught him to read and write and how to keep farm records. He became an excellent violinist and loved music. His father died when he was 14 years old, and Jefferson had to run a 2,500-acre farm. There were 30 slaves on the plantation who did most of the hard work, however.

When he was 16, Jefferson went to Williamsburg, Virginia's capital, to attend William and Mary College. Two of the professors there helped Jefferson learn social skills. The governor would join them some evenings, and the four of them talked and formed a musical quartet. After graduating, Jefferson prepared for a career as a lawyer with George Wythe. He had also taught Jefferson's cousin, John Marshall, who later became a chief justice of the Supreme Court. After his law practice became successful, Jefferson built his mansion and named it Monticello; he designed the house and gardens.

In 1772, he married Martha Skelton, a beautiful widow. Shortly after they married, her father died; her share of her father's estate was 40,000 acres and 135 slaves. Only two of the Jefferson's six children lived to be adults. Martha had poor health throughout their marriage, and she died in 1782.

During his lifetime, Jefferson studied a number of subjects, including Latin, Greek, Hebrew, Spanish, French, Indian languages, farming, geography, surveying, botany, theology, and medicine. He loved art and music and found comfort in playing his violin.

Jefferson had wealth, a profitable profession, and plenty to do with his time. But like others of his class, it was expected that he become involved in his community and his colony's affairs. He was elected to the House of Burgesses (lower house of the Virginia legislature) in 1769. He rarely gave speeches, but he became well known among the members for his ability to express complex ideas in simple English. This was an exciting time to be in the Virginia legislature, and he served with Patrick Henry, George Washington, and James Madison. Ill health forced Jefferson to miss the First Continental Congress, but he sent a long letter, later made public as "A Summary View..." In it, he attacked the king and Parliament for trying to tyrannize Americans.

As a delegate to the Second Continental Congress, he was named to the committee that was to write the Declaration of Independence. It is the most outstanding statement of human rights ever written. It says that rights do not come from government, but from God, and among those rights that cannot be taken by rulers are "life, liberty and the pursuit of happiness." The government's job is to protect those rights, and if it does not, the people have the duty to rebel and to form a new government.

He also attacked the established (tax-supported) church, arguing that the citizens should not be forced to attend church or pay taxes to support a particular church. Critics later charged that he was an atheist because of his Act for Establishing Religious Freedom. When the bill finally passed, he considered it one of the greatest achievements of his life.

From 1784 to 1789, he represented the United States in France. Jefferson liked many things about France, but was alarmed by the wealth of the French court and the poverty of the people. He understood the emotions behind the French Revolution and wrote: "I hold that a little rebellion now and then is a good thing." When he became secretary of state in 1789, Jefferson was the most pro-French member of the administration. Jefferson tired of the attacks on him by the Federalist newspapers, so he resigned from the cabinet in 1793.

In 1796, John Adams was elected president, barely beating Jefferson, who became vice president. After the Alien and Sedition Acts passed, Jefferson secretly wrote the Kentucky Resolution attacking them. Now, he and Adams were political enemies, each trying to win the presidency in 1800. In the election that year, Jefferson and his running mate, Aaron Burr, received the same number of electoral votes (73), because under the original Constitution, electors cast votes for president and vice president on the same ballot, and did not separate their choices for each office. That was corrected by the Twelfth Amendment. The House finally chose Jefferson for president on the thirty-sixth ballot.

JEFFERSON AS PRESIDENT. Jefferson said he preferred "a government rigorously frugal and simple," and he planned to pay off the national debt. He favored cutting the size of the army and navy; he wanted the navy to only patrol along the coastline and feared a standing army as dangerous to liberty. To calm fears he was going to get revenge on the Federalists, he said, "We are all Republicans, we are all Federalists."

One by one, his ideas were tossed aside. For example, when pirates started attacking American ships in the Mediterranean, he sent the navy and marines to punish their ruler at Tripoli.

The rise of Napoleon in France caused great fear among westerners, since France owned the region west of the Mississippi River. Jefferson sent James Monroe to join Robert Livingston, the ambassador in France, to see if the French were willing to sell New Orleans. Instead, they were told Napoleon was willing to sell all of Louisiana to the United States. The area included nearly all of the region from the west bank of the Mississippi River to the crest of the Rocky Mountains, an area equal in size to that east of the Mississippi River. The cost would be $15 million. Monroe and Livingston went far beyond what they had been told to do when they quickly signed the agreement in 1803; it was too good to pass up.

Jefferson also thought it was a great deal, but he worried about whether the Constitution allowed it. Most Federalists opposed buying this vast area because the people who settled there were likely to be Republicans. Some New Englanders even talked about seceding (leaving) the Union. Good sense prevailed, however, and it was approved. The United States was now 830,000 square miles larger.

Most of the region beyond the Mississippi River was unmapped, and had never been explored. This led to the Lewis and Clark expedition. Meriwether Lewis was Jefferson's personal secretary, and the president had often talked with him about a "journey of discovery" into the region. Lewis chose William Clark to be his co-leader for the trip. Their journey from 1804 to 1806 took them up the Missouri River and down the Snake and Columbia Rivers to the Pacific Coast. They mapped the region and reported their observations of animal and plant life, the course of rivers, Indians, and the weather. Their trip proved that it was possible to travel overland to the Pacific Coast.

In 1805, Zebulon Pike was sent to find the source of the Mississippi River, and afterward he traveled up the Arkansas River. He was captured by the Spanish when he wandered into their territory but persuaded them that it had been a mistake. He was held as a prisoner in Santa Fe for months, and was finally allowed to leave in 1807.

Jefferson disliked Vice President Burr, as did many others, including Alexander Hamilton. When he ran for governor of New York, Hamilton wrote a number of letters criticizing Burr's lack of morals and integrity. Burr challenged Hamilton to a duel in 1804, in which he killed Hamilton. Burr went into hiding after that, and began planning an expedition into the west. His exact purpose for taking an expedition down the Ohio and Mississippi Rivers isn't known, but it was suspected that he was trying to take land from the United States or Spain. He was arrested and taken to Richmond, Virginia, where he was tried before Chief Justice John Marshall. Jefferson made a great effort to get him convicted, but in the Constitution the definition of treason is so narrow that he escaped being punished.

Also during this time, the Supreme Court under the leadership of John Marshall began to expand its power. The Supreme Court had little power until it claimed the right to declare an act of Congress unconstitutional in the case of *Marbury v. Madison* in 1803.

Jefferson rejoiced when he retired and was "free to say and do what I please." He sometimes had 70 guests in his home at a time, and he was in poor financial shape when he died. He left his mark on the world as a thinker, shaper, and observer of America's growth from colonies into a nation extending two-thirds of the way across the continent.

LOUISIANA
PURCHASE
1803

Name: _____ Date: _____

Points to Ponder (Jefferson)

1. What were some of Jefferson's personal qualities that made him special?

   _____

   _____

2. What reasons might Jefferson have given for not going into politics in colonial Virginia?

   _____

   _____

3. It is said that the "pen is mightier than the sword." After reading the Declaration of Independence, what was its importance in proving that the statement is true?

   _____

   _____

   _____

4. Is it all right for a president to change his mind while he is in office, and do things much differently than he had stated during his campaign? Why or why not?

   _____

   _____

5. What made the *Marbury v. Madison* decision so important?

   _____

   _____

6. "When a man accepts a public trust, he should consider himself as public property." What does that statement by Jefferson mean to you?

   _____

   _____

☆ ☆ ☆ **Explore History** ☆ ☆ ☆

1. Make a poster or write a journal as if you traveled with the Lewis and Clark Expedition. Include pictures and descriptions of the animals, plant life, and any Indians you saw along the way. What did you eat? What type of supplies did you take along?

2. Thomas Jefferson was accomplished in many areas of learning. Write a report on the many subjects he studied. How did this knowledge contribute to his success?

JAMES MADISON
(1751–1836, P. 1809–1817)

People hardly noticed when James Madison entered a room; he was short, small, serious, and not distinguished in appearance. It was only when his wife, Dolley, walked in that they took notice. The losing candidate in 1808 said: "I was beaten by Mr. and Mrs. Madison. I might have had a better chance had I faced Mr. Madison alone."

Born into a wealthy Virginia planter's family, James was a sickly child. His mother taught him to read and write, and his father taught him the responsibility of public service. Their home was on the frontier, and he always remembered the war whoops of Indian warriors he had heard as a child. As a child, his playmates were the children of the family's slaves. When he was 11 years old, he was sent to study under a teacher who taught him French with a Scottish accent. After a few years there, a young minister became his tutor.

James attended Princeton University, graduating in 1771 after two years of study. Madison thought about becoming a minister, but he was a poor public speaker. As the Revolution came, he wanted to be involved but was too sickly to be a soldier. He played a minor role in the Virginia convention that called for independence and in the writing of the Virginia Declaration of Rights, which later became the model for the Bill of Rights.

He served in the Continental Congress as its youngest delegate in 1781, and he saw the need for a stronger government with the power to tax and regulate commerce. He was one of those involved in forming the Constitutional Convention in 1787, and his work there would have made him famous even if he had done nothing more.

Before the Convention began, Madison had been studying books and taking notes on ideas about government. He had three basic ideas: (1) the national government should draw its power from the people, not the states; (2) power should be spread out so no one has complete control; and (3) representation in Congress should be on the basis of population, not equal numbers from every state.

During the convention, Madison sat with his back to George Washington, the presiding officer, and took notes on what was being said. He promised that the notes would not be published until the last member of the Convention died. His role in debates and compromises at the Convention was so important he was later referred to as the "Father of the Constitution."

When the Constitution was sent to the states to be ratified, he played a major part. He teamed with John Jay and Alexander Hamilton in writing the Federalist Papers, which explained reasons for the Constitution's provisions. When Patrick Henry and others complained there were no guarantees of individual freedom in the Constitution, Madison said they would be added by amendment. As a member of the House, he proposed the amendments we know as the Bill of Rights. They were ratified by the states in 1789.

In debate, Madison lost the shyness and self-consciousness he often felt on other occasions. After someone stole his hat while he was staying at an inn, he refused to go out for two days fearing someone might see him without a hat. He was tongue-tied around women. When he was 30 years old, he fell in love for the first time with a 15-year-old girl. He felt humiliated when she suddenly broke off their engagement.

In 1794, he met Dolley Todd, a young widow. Soon, rumors spread that they were going to marry. The subject aroused so much interest that the Washingtons invited Dolley to their home. Washington told her it would be a lucky woman who won Madison. Later, Mrs. Washington suggested that James would make a fine husband, and if they did marry, she and her husband would approve. James and Dolley married three months after they met.

The Madison home became the center of social activity. When Dolley was disowned by the Quakers for marrying a non-Quaker, she began wearing bright colors, attending balls, and playing cards. Madison, who had always looked like a man going to a funeral, began to dance and socialize. An invitation to their home was highly prized.

In 1801, Thomas Jefferson chose Madison as secretary of state. Jefferson ran his own foreign policy, so there was little for Madison to do, but it was a good time to learn the ropes. The struggles between Great Britain and France made it difficult for American shipowners and sailors. The British blockaded the coastline of Europe, and France began seizing ships. American sailors were being taken from ships and impressed (forced to serve) on British ships. The worst incident was the *Chesapeake* Affair in 1807. The *Chesapeake* was a navy warship that was fired upon by a larger British ship, the *Leopard*. Three Americans were killed and 18 injured. The *Chesapeake* was then boarded, and four crew members were taken away. With a weak navy and strong disagreement on how to proceed, the United States was only able to stop trading with Europe by passing the Embargo Act.

Madison won the election of 1808 easily and became president in March 1809. Everyone noticed how much happier Jefferson was than Madison at the inauguration.

MADISON AS PRESIDENT. Nothing the United States tried improved relations with Great Britain or France. Since the British were able to restrict Americans more than the French, Americans were angrier with the British. Another problem for Madison arose when Indians, led by Tecumseh and the Prophet with British help, were threatening the frontier. General William Henry Harrison defeated the Indians at Tippecanoe Creek. It was discovered that some weapons left behind on the battlefield had been made in England.

In 1811, a pro-war faction took over Congress. Led by Speaker of the House Henry Clay, they were labeled "War Hawks" by a critic and soon proudly called themselves by that name. Madison was not enthusiastic about fighting the British, but when public pressure demanded it, he gave in. New England bitterly opposed what they called "Mr. Madison's War."

The United States was not prepared for war against the strongest navy and one of the largest armies in the world. There was little money in the treasury, and the War Department was badly run. Despite many failures, however, there were some successes that raised the nation's spirits. Commodore Oliver Perry defeated a British fleet on Lake Erie. At the Battle of the Thames, General Harrison's troops killed Tecumseh while defeating a British-Indian force. General Andrew Jackson was successful in his battle with Creek Indians at Horseshoe Bend. The British fleet on Lake Champlain was defeated by Thomas Macdonough's squadron.

In 1814, a British fleet landed troops near Washington, D.C. An army to oppose them was quickly gathered but fled soon after the British opened fire. When Dolley was told the British were coming, she quickly gathered some important papers and had a worker take down a portrait of Washington before she left the Executive Mansion. After the British drank the hot tea still on the table, they burned the president's home, the Capitol building, and the Library of Congress. They then moved on to Baltimore, which was defended by Fort McHenry. Seeing the American flag still flying in the morning inspired Francis Scott Key to write "The Star-Spangled Banner," which was later set to music.

Many Federalist hotheads opposed the war from the beginning. Secretly meeting at the Hartford Convention in 1814, they drew up a number of demands, which included that no two consecutive presidents could come from the same state and no declaration of war would be allowed unless the United States was actually invaded. Before they arrived in Washington to present their demands, the war ended, and the committee returned home to be ridiculed by the public.

The Treaty of Ghent ended the war with no winners or losers. Before the treaty arrived from Ghent, a British force attacked General Jackson's defenses at New Orleans. The British lost 2,600 men, while only eight Americans were killed and 13 wounded. It made Americans more proud of their country than ever. Madison's popularity had never been higher, which helped his friend, the new president, James Monroe.

Madison retired to his home, Montpelier, in Virginia and spent the rest of his life as a gentleman farmer and rector of the University of Virginia. He worked for the abolition of slavery and advised President Monroe on foreign policy issues. He died in 1836.

After his death, Dolley returned to Washington to live. To pay off her son's gambling debts, she sold Montpelier. She was still very popular, and important people looked forward to spending an evening with her. She did some entertaining, but financial problems caused her to limit her receptions to only one each month. She died in 1849.

Name: _____ Date: _____

Points to Ponder (Madison)

1. What might your opinion of young James Madison have been?

   _____

   _____

2. After reading Article I of the Constitution, which house of Congress is closest to Madison's idea of proportional representation? Why?

   _____

   _____

3. Why was marrying Dolley so important to his career?

   _____

   _____

   _____

4. What did the "War Hawks" want?

   _____

   _____

5. Who were two heroes of the war who later became presidents?

   _____

6. What do you think happened to the Federalists after the public found out about the Hartford Convention?

   _____

   _____

⭐ ⭐ ⭐ **Explore History** ⭐ ⭐ ⭐

1. Write a mini-report about the impressment of sailors and the *Chesapeake* Affair. Describe the connection to the War of 1812.

2. Write a short biography on Francis Scott Key or Dolley Madison. Include a picture. Share your knowledge with the class.

3. Make a poster of the Bill of Rights. Include a brief description of each amendment and what it means to you as an American.

JAMES MONROE
(1758–1831, P. 1817–1825)

The nation, so divided during the war, went through an amazing change afterwards. People who had thought of themselves only as New Yorkers or Georgians before the war were now Americans first. The grumpy Federalists who had opposed the War of 1812 were now either Republicans or keeping their views silent. In 1817, a Boston newspaper called this the "Era of Good Feeling," and the name stuck. The man receiving the most advantage of this new era was James Monroe, the fifth president of the United States.

The Monroes were respectable farmers with good connections. James's uncle was a friend of Washington, Jefferson, and Madison. James was educated at home at first, then walked miles to the school of Reverend Archibald Campbell with his friend and neighbor, John Marshall. In 1774, he went to Williamsburg to study at William and Mary College, but these were not times for books and lessons. Trouble with Great Britain caused the students to form militia units, and he was made a lieutenant in a Virginia regiment. The regiment was sent to New York to support Washington's army. By the time they arrived, New York was lost, and the army was in retreat. Then came the surprise attack on Trenton. In the battle there, Monroe was wounded and put out of action for two months. He was then promoted to captain.

In 1777, after the Battle of Brandywine, he and the Frenchman Lafayette became close friends. After the attack on Germantown, Monroe was promoted to major. With a lull in the fighting, he returned to Virginia and studied law under Thomas Jefferson. They became friends for life.

In 1782, Monroe was elected to the Virginia legislature, and in the next year, he was appointed to serve in the Confederation Congress. After he returned in 1785, he started his law practice and served at the Virginia convention ratifying the U.S. Constitution. In 1790, he was chosen for the U.S. Senate, where he often argued against Washington policies. In 1794, George Washington made him minister (ambassador) to France. It was hoped he could improve U.S. relations with France, which were in poor shape at the time. His pro-French views were not in line with Washington's policy of neutrality in the struggles between Great Britain and France, and Monroe was recalled (fired) in 1796. He and Washington were quite angry with each other after that, and they never reconciled their differences.

From 1799 to 1802, Monroe was governor of Virginia. From 1803 to 1807, he was most often overseas on diplomatic missions. He worked with Livingston on the Louisiana Purchase, tried to get Spain to give up East and West Florida, and failed to get Great Britain to stop impressing (seizing) American sailors. After the *Chesapeake* Affair ended, along with any chance for a treaty with Great Britain, Monroe returned to the United States in 1807. He served again in the Virginia legislature in 1810 and as governor in 1811.

President Madison chose Monroe to be secretary of state in 1811, where he served in that capacity until 1817. It was a difficult time; the United States went into a war, fought it, and had to make peace. Although the treaty did not include impressment of sailors in its terms, the treaty was signed by the American negotiators. When Americans heard the news of Jackson's victory at New Orleans at almost the same time the treaty came back from Europe, they assumed that the English had given in because of the battle. However, the battle actually took place two weeks after the treaty was signed. Madison had never been as popular as he was then.

Monroe's victory in 1816 was one of the easiest ever. The Federalist candidate had practically no support, and only three states cast votes for him. The "Era of Good Feeling" had begun. In 1820, only one elector did not vote for Monroe, saying that only Washington deserved to be elected unanimously. The good feelings lasted for about six years.

MONROE AS PRESIDENT. The United States was growing rapidly during Monroe's presidency. As before, the president's main job was in handling foreign affairs. The United States had gained respect during the War of 1812, and Great Britain had no desire to tangle with her American cousins again. In 1817, the two nations agreed to take their navies off the Great Lakes. There, the only armed ships were to be customs boats to collect taxes. In 1818, the United States-Canada boundary between the Lake of the Woods and the crest of the Rocky Mountains was settled at the forty-ninth parallel.

The United States had long wanted Spanish Florida, which at that time extended from the Atlantic Ocean along a narrow strip reaching Baton Rouge, Louisiana. Many rivers flowed southward into that strip. Southerners feared Spain might stop them from using those rivers to get their crops to market. Americans who lived in Florida wanted to take it from Spain. In 1810, they captured the region west of the Pearl River, and in 1813, the region west of the Perdido River was taken. The Spanish protested, but since they were involved in a war, they could do nothing to stop it.

Revolutions were breaking out in Latin America, and many Americans wanted to help those colonies overthrow Spain. There were others who wanted to see the U.S. flag flying over East Florida. Secretary of State John Q. Adams worried that a rash move might lead to war not only with Spain, but also with those kingdoms who were friendly with Spain.

Florida had become the nesting place for many groups hostile to the United States. Seminole Indians raided Georgia farms and then returned to Florida before they could be caught; pirates used it as a base; the British troops who had been defeated at New Orleans hid there. The Spanish were too weak to stop these groups or punish them. General Andrew Jackson was sent to stop Indian attacks and to cross into Florida if necessary. His written orders said he was not to attack Spanish towns or forts. Jackson said later that he had secret instructions to seize Spanish towns; Monroe denied it.

Jackson did not like Indians, Spaniards, or Englishmen. He caught two Englishmen, found them guilty of stirring up Indians against the United States, and executed them. By the time he was finished, all of Florida except St. Augustine was in his hands.

Jackson returned to Tennessee as a hero to westerners. Those in Congress who saw Jackson as a future political foe wanted him punished. Great Britain and Spain both protested his actions, but after looking at the evidence, the British decided the two Englishmen deserved their fate.

Monroe and nearly the entire cabinet thought Jackson should be punished for going beyond orders. His only defender in the room was Secretary of State Adams who now favored a get-tough policy with Spain. Jackson's strong public support made it easy to convince the cabinet and Monroe that Adams was right. Adams told the Spanish that they should have controlled the

Indians and demanded that their officials in Florida be punished. A treaty was signed giving the United States all of Florida.

Two new problems were developing. The Russians owned Alaska and warned foreign ships not to come near it. They also planned to move down the Pacific Coast into Oregon Country (which the United States and Great Britain had already claimed). Most Americans had no interest in a place as far-off as Oregon, but Monroe and Adams knew they must stop this move.

Some European rulers talked of working together to stop threats against their power. The United States worried that the Europeans might invade Latin America and put down the revolutions there. In 1823's State of the Union message to Congress, Monroe stated what came to be forever known as the Monroe Doctrine. It warned Europe not to expand to acquire colonies in North or South America. It also said the United States was not going to get involved in European problems. Some Europeans protested, but Great Britain was not going to let them interfere with the trade they had developed there, so Spain and other countries could do nothing except complain.

A major domestic problem arose when Missouri was being considered for statehood. Missouri allowed slavery, and some in Congress wanted to keep it from becoming a state unless it would limit slavery in the future. This led to the Missouri Compromise. Missouri was allowed to enter as a slave state, while Maine entered as a free state. Slavery would be forbidden in the Louisiana Purchase territories north of the 36°30′ line of latitude. The argument over the Missouri Compromise was the first serious struggle over slavery; however, it was not to be the last.

In personal relations, Monroe usually got along well with people, but there were exceptions. In an argument with Secretary of the Treasury William H. Crawford, he told Crawford his language was improper and unsuitable. Crawford raised his cane as if to strike the president, and said: "You infernal scoundrel!" Monroe grabbed the tongs from the fireplace to protect himself and said he would ring for the servants to drive Crawford from the house. Crawford calmed down and said he had intended no insult; however, they never met again.

The Monroes did not entertain in the grand style of Dolley Madison, and Elizabeth Monroe was criticized for not doing more. She was not in good health and was a quiet, reserved person. They finally began entertaining but were again criticized because instead of a few high officials, the people they invited were secretaries, farmers, ministers, bookkeepers, and merchants. Many were dirty and their hair was uncombed.

When Monroe left office, he was as popular as ever; however, the party was splitting apart as rivals rushed to replace him. This led to the brutal struggle for the presidency in 1824.

Name: _____ Date: _____

Points to Ponder (Monroe)

1. Why was Monroe's presidency called the "Era of Good Feeling"?

   _____

   _____

2. During the Revolution, in what battle was Monroe wounded?

   _____

3. What political offices in Virginia did Monroe hold during his career?

   _____

   _____

   _____

4. What problems did the United States and Great Britain settle after the War of 1812?

   _____

   _____

   _____

5. Why did Jackson invade East Florida? With what two nations did his invasion cause trouble? Why wasn't he punished?

   _____

   _____

   _____

6. What did the Monroe Doctrine say? _____

   _____

   _____

★ ★ ★ **Explore History** ★ ★ ★

1. Draw or construct a map of free and slave states at the time of the Missouri Compromise. Make the free states a different color from the slave states.

2. James Monroe was chosen as President Madison's secretary of state. Which other presidents served in this position?

3. Write a report on the history of Florida. How many countries claimed ownership throughout its history? During Monroe's presidency, why did the United States want it so badly?

JOHN QUINCY ADAMS
(1767–1848, P. 1825–1829)

One writer described John Quincy Adams as a "chip off the old family glacier." He was a hard worker, with devotion to his country, unusual travel opportunities, and intelligence as an important part of his record. The circumstances by which he became president, his poor understanding of politics, having ideas too advanced for his time, and poor social skills were the curses of his years as president.

He was the oldest son of President John Adams. While Quincy (as he was often called) was growing up, his father was away serving in the Continental Congress. When he was 11, he begged to go with his father to Europe and was given permission. He attended schools in Paris, Amsterdam, and Leyden. At the age of 14, he became a private secretary to the American minister (ambassador) to Russia. In 1783, he became his father's private secretary. Two years later, he returned to the United States to study at Harvard College. He graduated in 1787, read law for three years, and became a lawyer.

In 1794, Washington chose John Quincy Adams as minister to Holland. The French invaded three days after he arrived, so he went to London, where he met Louisa Johnson, who later became his wife. It was not a happy marriage. He insisted that she do everything his way, and she had a mind of her own. She was often sad and lonely and resented his being away so often. As the president's wife, she was an excellent hostess and made everyone feel comfortable. In their later years, they found happiness working in the anti-slavery and women's rights movements together.

From 1794 to 1801, Adams was away from the United States serving as minister to Holland, Portugal, Prussia, and Sweden. Adams served in the U.S. Senate from 1803 to 1808, and then as minister to Russia (1809–1814). From 1815 to 1817, he was minister to Great Britain. After that, he did an outstanding job as Monroe's secretary of state. His ability was shown in his handling of the Florida situation and the Monroe Doctrine. These events made him one of the very best secretaries of state in history.

As the Monroe administration neared the end of its term, 17 ambitious politicians decided they were best qualified to replace him. Politics became a cutthroat game as leaders tried to eliminate competition. Andrew Jackson from Tennessee was a war hero, Adams was secretary of state, William H. Crawford was secretary of the treasury, Henry Clay was Speaker of the House, and John C. Calhoun was secretary of war. Calhoun saw that the field was too crowded, so he ran for vice president; there was no competition for that job. Now there were four candidates. Crawford suffered a stroke that left him nearly blind and helpless for several weeks, which then left three active candidates.

When the election of 1824 took place, Jackson received the most electoral votes, Adams was second, Crawford was third, and Clay was fourth. The Twelfth Amendment says if no candidate for president has a clear majority, the House must choose from the top three. The struggle now was between Jackson and Adams. Clay threw his support behind Adams after they held a secret meeting. Adams won over the protest of many Americans who believed Jackson should have won.

JOHN QUINCY ADAMS AS PRESIDENT. Trouble for the new president began when he appointed Henry Clay as his secretary of state. When Jackson heard the news, he was furious. He suspected that a deal had been made between Adams and Clay and let everyone know how he felt. His followers were vocal and many. There were more anti-Adams members in Congress than pro-Adams.

Instead of playing politics and building a band of loyal supporters, Adams tried to rise above politics as Washington had. Many in the administration found it easy to work against him, including the vice president and many cabinet members. Adams had many grand projects in mind, but every time he suggested something, his opponents, who labeled themselves the "Opposition," made fun of it and then killed his idea.

Adams wanted to build 130 astronomical observatories. He called them "lighthouses of the sky." Many jokes were made about this idea, which in the view of many was a waste of thousands of dollars. He proposed creating a department of the interior and a national university, but they were killed for the same reason. He wanted the federal government to pay for internal improvements (roads and canals), but Congress turned that idea into a way to fund favorite projects to please the voters back home.

Adams wanted to treat the Creek Indians in Georgia fairly, but the governor was determined to drive them out. The issue was not settled until after Adams left office, and the new president, Andrew Jackson, came in. An Indian hater, he sided with Georgia against the Creeks.

Adams could not even enjoy the comfort of a billiard table and chess set without controversy. He paid $61 for a billiard table and $23.50 for a chess set out of his own pocket. Opponents said he bought them with public money, and they "proved" that he was a gambler. He also enjoyed early morning swims in the Potomac and would shed all his clothes and dive in. Once his clothes were stolen, and he paid a boy to bring some fresh clothes from the White House. Another time, a woman reporter sat on his clothes and refused to leave until he gave her an interview.

Henry Clay made great efforts to send two delegates to a meeting of Latin American countries that was to be held in Panama. Critics came out to attack the idea (most were opposed to anything Clay proposed), but he finally got the approval of Congress. One delegate died before he arrived, and the other was on his way when he found out that the meeting was over, and so returned home.

A high tariff passed in Congress in 1828 with help from the Northeast. The South opposed it, and the split between North and South caused resentment that would bring on a future crisis.

Nothing Adams proposed was going to be successful. As his term came to a close in 1828, his enemies turned to General Andrew Jackson as his replacement. Adams thought Jackson was totally incapable of being president, but the public disagreed; they elected Jackson by a vote of 178 to 83 electoral votes. A bitter John Quincy Adams left town in the morning before Jackson's noon inauguration.

In 1831, Adams was elected to the House from a Massachusetts district and served there until 1848. While there, he worked in the anti-slavery cause and for better treatment of women. He died as he wanted to—at his desk.

Name: _____ Date: _____

Points to Ponder (J.Q. Adams)

1. What was unusual about the school days of John Q. Adams?

   _____

   _____

2. Was his early career in government helpful in understanding American politics? Why or why not?

   _____

   _____

3. Do you think that, under the circumstances, it helped Clay's career when he accepted the job of secretary of state? Why or why not?

   _____

   _____

   _____

4. Why do you think Adams left office a bitter man at the end of his term?

   _____

   _____

5. President Truman suggested that former presidents should be given a non-voting seat in the Senate because they have had unique experiences. What do you think Adams might have added to the House by being a former president?

   _____

   _____

   _____

⭐ ⭐ ⭐ **Explore History**   ⭐ ⭐ ⭐

1. John Q. Adams traveled extensively as a young man, both as a student and as ambassador. Draw a map of his travels or write a journal about the sights he may have seen in Europe.

2. Following his term as president, John Q. Adams worked in the anti-slavery cause and for the better treatment of women. Stage a class debate on one of these topics.

3. Adams tried to treat the Creek Indians fairly, but Andrew Jackson hated Indians. Write a mini-report on the Creek Indians and how they were treated during this period.

ANDREW JACKSON
(1767–1845, P. 1829–1837)

On the evening before the inauguration of the seventh president, New England ministers held prayer vigils, President Adams was busy boxing up his books and personal items so he could leave in the morning, and Secretary of State Henry Clay nervously paced as the clock ticked off the seconds. However, not everyone was worried. Men and women from Tennessee and Kentucky had come to Washington to celebrate and to witness their hero taking the oath of office. Tomorrow a great change was coming, and while no one knew what would happen when Andrew Jackson became president, they knew things were going to be different.

Andrew was the third son of poor immigrants from Northern Ireland, and he was the first president born in a log cabin. His father died before he was born, and his mother moved in with a sister who had eight children. It was a noisy house with each child having to defend himself. Andrew was a fighter, and even when someone had him down, he refused to give up. He joined the militia during the Revolution and became a messenger at the age of 13. His two brothers died during the war, one killed in battle, and the other dying of smallpox. Andrew was captured, and when a British officer ordered him to clean his boots, Andrew refused. The soldier struck at Andrew with his sword, slashing him across the hand and face, scarring him for life. His mother died while nursing soldiers on a prison ship. Andrew was alone in the world at the age of 14.

Jackson became wild and reckless, wasting the money that he had inherited from his grandfather on horse races and cock fights. He did not even stop his wild ways while he studied to be a lawyer. He was intelligent, however, and passed the bar exam, becoming a lawyer at age 20. When a friend of Jackson's was appointed as judge in what is now Tennessee, he appointed Jackson as solicitor (prosecuting attorney) in Nashville. He built up a good law practice on the side; he also fell in love.

While living at the boardinghouse of the widowed Mrs. John Donelson, Jackson met Mrs. Rachel Robards, whose husband was an army captain and rarely at home. When Captain Robards came home, there were quarrels, and he filed for divorce. Thinking the divorce had been granted, Jackson married Rachel in 1791. It was not until December 1793 that the Jacksons learned that the divorce had gone through only in September of that year, so they remarried in January 1794. Jackson was very protective of his wife, and he warned one and all that they would suffer if anything bad was said about her.

Nashville was growing rapidly, and Jackson made a small fortune buying land for ten cents an acre and selling it for $3. In 1796, he bought the Hermitage, a plantation a few miles from Nashville. He also went into politics, serving in the state constitutional convention, the U.S. House in 1796, and the Senate in 1797. He was elected to the state supreme court and served on it for six years. While he was holding court in a small town, the town bully was causing trouble outside. The sheriff was afraid of the man and could not stop him, so Jackson grabbed two guns and faced the man. The man meekly surrendered and went to jail. When asked why he had given up so easily, the man said that when he had looked into Jackson's eyes, he saw "shoot" and knew it was "time to sing small, and so I did."

Jackson's reputation for dueling was first made in 1806 when he shot and killed a man famous for his ability with pistols. The man fired, hitting Jackson in the chest. Jackson then fired, killing his opponent. There were more duels to follow. Jackson was simply following his mother's advice: "Never sue for assault or slander; settle them cases yourself."

Jackson had been major general of the Tennessee militia since 1802. When the War of 1812 came, he was anxious to fight. He received orders to move his troops to New Orleans in 1813. Even before his 2,500 men had arrived, they were ordered to return home. He led his men back through 500 miles of rough land. He walked so a sick soldier could ride on his horse. One of his men commented that Jackson was as tough as hickory, and after that, he was often called by the nickname, "Old Hickory."

During the War of 1812, Jackson became famous for two battles. He attacked the Creek Indians (British allies) at Horseshoe Bend. After allowing women and children to leave, he attacked, killing 800 men. One of those wounded in the battle was Sam Houston, who later became leader of the Texas Revolution. The other battle occurred in January 1815, two weeks after the peace treaty was signed. At New Orleans, Jackson, along with his army comprised of frontiersmen, pirates, and shop clerks, defeated a well-trained British army.

In 1817, Jackson was ordered to stop Indian attacks in Spanish Florida. His army created an international squabble when he executed two British subjects for encouraging Indian attacks, and he took control of all Florida except St. Augustine. Many easterners were not pleased, but his reputation grew in the West by leaps and bounds. He refused to run against Monroe, but came close to winning the election of 1824. His narrow defeat was only temporary, and in 1828, he was eager to run again.

The campaign of 1828 was the most malicious the nation had ever seen. To Jackson followers, it was the common people against the aristocrats. To Adams supporters, it was respectable people against the mob. Neither side held back in attacking the other. Among charges against Jackson were that he was a murderer, bigamist, slave trader, drunkard, and thief, but it was the attacks on his wife that hurt Jackson the most. When Rachel died in December, he blamed it on John Q. Adams and Henry Clay. Since all but two states chose electors by popular vote now, the election was a good test of public opinion. Jackson received 647,000 votes to Adams's 508,000. The electoral vote was more one-sided, 178–83.

JACKSON AS PRESIDENT. A large crowd showed up for the inaugural address, but few could hear Jackson's words. After the ceremonies, the crowd went over to the reception at the White House. No preparation had been made for the large numbers packing the rooms. Dishes, glasses, and furniture were destroyed, and to avoid being injured in the crush, Jackson climbed out a window and spent the day at a boardinghouse nearby. To his enemies it seemed King Mob had taken over.

Jackson chose his cabinet to run the executive departments, but he was more inclined to listen to an informal group of friends that were soon called the "Kitchen Cabinet." They were too clever to tell him what he "must" do, but they definitely influenced his thinking. Only Secretary of State Martin Van Buren was an important voice from the cabinet.

Among the major events of his administration, five will be briefly discussed here.

1. "The spoils system." Jackson supporters wanted the jobs that Adams's officials had; the old expression, "To the victor belong the spoils" led to the nickname: "the spoils system." While Jackson expected his new officials to work hard, some did not, and others were simply unable to do their jobs. While it seemed that every Adams appointee was fired, it was closer to 10 to 20 percent who were dismissed.

2. The Eaton affair resulted from Jackson's defense of a woman's virtue and memories of the political attacks on his own wife. It began when Secretary of War John Eaton fell in love with a married woman, Peggy Timberlake. Her husband died, and rumors spread that he had killed himself because his wife was unfaithful. Eaton wanted to marry Peggy, but he checked with Jackson first. Jackson admired her, and he supported Eaton. The ladies of Washington were scandalized, and led by Floride Calhoun, wife of the vice president, they refused to socialize with Mrs. Eaton. Van Buren saw an opportunity to please Jackson in this, and he arranged dinner parties with the Eatons. Van Buren used this social issue as a wedge he could drive between Jackson and Vice President John C. Calhoun.

3. The nullification issue. The South was worried by the growth of population in the North and its effect on the future. With more electoral votes, the North could choose future presidents, and their numbers would increase in the House. If more northern states came into the Union, the South would lose the Senate too. The South devised nullification as the answer to this problem. If Congress passed a law a state did not like, it could "nullify" it and keep it from being enforced inside its borders. If the federal government tried to enforce the law, the state would secede (leave) from the Union.

In 1830, a hot debate occurred in the Senate over this issue between Senator Robert Hayne of South Carolina and Senator Daniel Webster of Massachusetts. Webster said that the federal government was created by the people, not the states, and national interest was more important than the desires of any state or section. Jackson's position was unknown until the Jefferson Day dinner in 1830. After the program that night, Jackson offered the first toast: "Our Union, it must be preserved." Calhoun feebly gave the next toast: "The Union, next to our liberty, most dear."

After the election of 1832, which Jackson easily won, South Carolina declared the high tariffs (taxes on imports) unconstitutional and threatened to secede if the government tried to collect these new tariffs in their state. Jackson was furious, and he sent troops and naval ships to Fort Sumter in Charleston harbor. Congress gave him the power to use force to collect the taxes. Hayne resigned his Senate seat to become governor, and Calhoun resigned as vice president to become senator. Senator Henry Clay proposed that the tariff be cut as a compromise. South Carolina withdrew the nullification of the tariff, and troops were not needed to enforce it.

The election of 1832 is important because a national convention was first used to choose candidates. Jackson opponents, calling themselves "National Republicans" at the time, chose Clay for president, and the "Democratic Republicans" chose Jackson for president and Van Buren for vice president. The big issue of the campaign was whether to re-charter the Second Bank of the United States.

4. The Bank issue. In 1816, the Second Bank of the United States was chartered for 20 years. It was very powerful, and many people didn't like it. Small banks in the West did not like limits on lending, and those wanting to borrow were angry when they could not get a loan. The

Bank gave money to those running for office to use in their campaigns; therefore, many in the House and Senate did not want the Bank to go out of business. In 1832, Clay and Webster proposed a bill that would re-charter the Bank, even though the charter would not run out for four more years. They hoped it would split the pro-Jackson forces, and make it possible for Clay to be elected. Jackson vetoed the bill, and when he won the election, he began taking government money out of the Bank and putting it into state banks.

5. Indian removal. Jackson did not like Indians, and did not want them on valuable farm land in the East. He wanted them moved west of the Mississippi River. Congress gave him the power to trade land in the west for land in the east, and unfair treaties were forced on Indians to get them to move. The Indians suffered greatly during this process. The Cherokees called the trip the "Trail of Tears" because so many died. The Seminoles moved deeper into the Everglades of Florida and fought many years before most of them finally gave up. The Eastern Indians were settled in Indian Territory (now Oklahoma).

After his two terms ended in 1837, Jackson moved back to his home at the Hermitage. Andrew Jackson had opened the door of politics for others who came from poor families. The election of Jackson made America more democratic. People realized that if those in office did not listen to their complaints and desires, they could vote that officeholder and his party out of office.

Name: _____ Date: _____

Points to Ponder (Jackson)

1. How did Jackson get a scar on his face and hand?

   _____

   _____

2. Bigamy is being married to two people at the same time. Why did Jackson's opponents refer to Mrs. Jackson as a bigamist? Was it a fair accusation?

   _____

   _____

   What happened to Mrs. Jackson in the campaign of 1828 that caused Jackson to hate his opponents?

   _____

   _____

3. How did Jackson get the nickname "Old Hickory"?

   _____

   _____

4. What is meant by "the spoils system"? _____

   _____

   _____

5. If states could nullify acts of Congress, what would happen to the federal government's power?

   _____

   _____

   _____

☆ ☆ ☆ **Explore History** ☆ ☆ ☆

1. Draw a map of the "Trail of Tears," or write a journal about the journey. Where did the Indians settle? What hardships along the way caused so many to perish?

2. "Remember the Alamo!" Pretend you are a reporter or an eyewitness during the Texas War for Independence. Report what you see, or interview Santa Anna or Sam Houston. Write a news article and include a picture.

MARTIN VAN BUREN
(1782–1862, P. 1837–1841)

Martin Van Buren was one of the most skilled political leaders of his time. He had worked hard in behalf of Andrew Jackson and had designed his political campaign in 1832. It had brought him the vice presidency in 1833 and the presidency in 1837. But in 1840, the methods he developed were used against him by his opponent.

Martin Van Buren was born in 1782 in Kinderhook, New York, the son of a small farm and tavern owner. The family belonged to the Dutch Reformed Church and owned slaves. After a few years of schooling, Martin got a job working as janitor for a local Federalist lawyer. When Martin made it clear he was for Jefferson, he was fired. He then moved to New York where he studied law under a good Republican. "Little Van," (he was only 5′6″ tall) as he was known, became a lawyer in 1803. He had become careful about what he said, and he never spoke on any subject until he was sure which way the political winds were blowing. A reporter once asked him if the sun rose in the east. He said he was not sure since he did not rise that early.

Martin had married a woman distantly related to him in 1807, but she died 18 years before he became president. Little is known about her except that she was kindhearted and quiet. He never remarried. Politics was more important to him than any woman would be. In 1812, Van Buren was elected to the New York senate where he supported construction of the Erie Canal and favored abolishing imprisonment for debt.

Van Buren was one of the first politicians to realize the press could be made a valuable ally, and he used the *Argus* in New York and the *Globe* in Washington to get his party's message out. In 1821, he was chosen for the U.S. Senate, but he kept close watch on New York politics through his party organization, the Albany Regency. The Regency rewarded friends with jobs and punished party officeholders who did not obey its policies. Through the Regency, Van Buren controlled New York politics for many years.

In 1824, Van Buren worked in the William H. Crawford campaign for president, but when John Quincy Adams won, he organized political support among the Adams opposition. In 1828, he gave up his Senate seat to run for governor. He came up with the slogan that helped Jackson win: "John Quincy Adams, who can write," and "Andrew Jackson, who can fight."

When Jackson was elected, he appointed Van Buren as secretary of state. Van Buren had been governor less than three months, but he resigned to take the job. Since foreign governments were alarmed that a man of Jackson's background could be president, it was Van Buren's job to calm their fears. His good manners and stylish clothing appealed to them, so he was able to improve American relations with other countries.

Van Buren's main activity was not foreign affairs, however, but winning Jackson over. He began by cutting Vice President Calhoun out of Jackson's circle of friends. Then he did whatever was necessary to please Jackson. He rode horseback with Jackson early in the morning, when he hated riding horses. He said things he was sure would get back to Jackson. He told Peggy

Eaton that he had studied great men, and the greatest man of all was Jackson. She told Jackson, and he was very pleased.

In 1832, Van Buren was chosen as Jackson's running mate. The Whigs did what they could to embarrass him, but Van Buren remained cool and calm. When Jackson came to choose his successor, Van Buren was the only name on the list. The Democrats chose him as their candidate for president in 1836. The Whigs ran three candidates against him; Van Buren won with 170 electoral votes. The Whig who ran closest in the electoral count was William Henry Harrison, the hero of Tippecanoe and governor of Indiana Territory. Now, "Old Kinderhook" was to be president.

VAN BUREN AS PRESIDENT. When Van Buren took the oath of office in 1837, he was most concerned about the growth of abolitionism. The abolitionists opposed slavery, and Van Buren feared they would split North from South. The best-known abolitionist was William Lloyd Garrison, whose newspaper, the *Liberator,* was very controversial. Van Buren said Congress should not interfere with slavery in the states or the District of Columbia.

After slaves who were illegally captured in Africa took over the Spanish ship *L'Amistad,* Van Buren wanted the slaves sent back to their Spanish owners. When a district court found in favor of the slaves, the government appealed the case to the U.S. Supreme Court. Defending the slaves was former President John Q. Adams; the Court declared they were free men.

In his inaugural address, Van Buren painted a glowing picture of the future. It did not take long, however, for the sunshine he predicted to turn into a thunderstorm of closed factories, large numbers of unemployed, and farmers losing their land because of unpaid debts.

The Panic of 1837 was the result of an economy expanding too quickly, with people borrowing money at outrageous interest. In Michigan, one man was paying 75 percent interest on money he had borrowed to buy land. In the New York City area, land prices doubled and tripled in short periods of time. States were borrowing money to build railroads and canals. Without the Second Bank of the United States to stop over-lending, the country was in crisis.

Van Buren had ignored warnings of troubles ahead. When he did show concern, it was for the welfare of the government, not the individuals who were suffering. Rather than risk losing its deposits in state banks, the Treasury Department was to take its money out of those banks and put it into an Independent Treasury.

The Whigs (now the official name of the party opposing the Democrats) were led by Henry Clay and Daniel Webster. They said the government should work to save the economy. The financial crisis eased somewhat in 1838, but the weak economy badly hurt Van Buren's chances of re-election in 1840. When he left the White House, he said he agreed with Jefferson that the happiest two days of his life were when he entered office and when he surrendered it.

In 1844, Van Buren tried to win the Democratic nomination, but he was not seriously considered because he opposed annexing Texas, a slave state. By 1848, he was firmly anti-slavery. Since he was not seeking public office any longer, he could travel to Europe and live in the high style he preferred. He died in 1862.

Like Herbert Hoover later, Van Buren had the misfortune of spending most of his time as president fighting off an economic panic that simply did not go away.

Name: _____ Date: _____

Points to Ponder (Van Buren)

1. What was the Albany Regency? _____

_____

_____

2. Why do you think Van Buren switched from Crawford to Jackson? What job did Jackson give him?

_____

_____

_____

3. What caused the Panic of 1837? What concerned Van Buren the most about it?

_____

_____

_____

4. When hard times hit the nation, is the president blamed for it? Do you think the president deserves all the blame when hard times come?

_____

_____

_____

5. Why did Van Buren oppose annexing Texas in 1844? How had his views changed from what they had been earlier?

_____

_____

_____

★ ★ ★ **Explore History** ★ ★ ★

1. Van Buren "courted" the media. His manners and appearance helped his appeal. Pretend you are at a press conference. What questions would you ask him about the issues of his administration? How did the media in Van Buren's time compare or differ from today?

2. The best-known abolitionist of Van Buren's time was William Lloyd Garrison, whose newspaper was the *Liberator*. Imagine that you are a slave owner and write an editorial opposing his views.

3. Write a short biography on Daniel Webster.

WILLIAM HENRY HARRISON
(1773–1841, P. 1841)

In 1828, the Democrats had won by claiming their candidate was a man of the people, while the opponent lived in great luxury. In 1840, the Whigs used that same image to defeat the Democrat in office.

William Henry Harrison was born in a three-story mansion into a wealthy Virginia family. He was tutored at home, then graduated from Hampden-Sidney College. He was first interested in a medical career but switched to the army infantry. In 1795, he married the daughter of a wealthy farmer and built her a log cabin. This log cabin later became part of a larger home, but it would become important as part of his presidential campaign years later.

In 1799, Harrison was the Northwest Territory's delegate to Congress, and he convinced Congress to separate Ohio and Indiana. He was appointed by President Adams as governor of the Indiana Territory in 1800. Earlier he had opposed slavery, but now he took the more popular view that slavery was legal and citizens should have the right to own slaves. It is believed that he changed his views to suit those of most people in the Territory.

Harrison's main problem was persuading Indians to give up their land so whites could settle on the land. Tecumseh and his younger brother, who was called "the Prophet," were busy organizing the Indians to fight against giving their land away. The Prophet was a reformed drunkard who had been converted by the Shakers. He was short, ugly, and one-eyed. He claimed to be a prophet, and his followers believed he could do anything. It was Tecumseh, however, who was a truly great leader. When Harrison met him, he said that had he lived in another time, Tecumseh would have been the founder of an empire that would have rivaled the glory of Peru or Mexico.

In 1811, Harrison formed an army of 1,000 men and moved toward the Indian camp at Tippecanoe. After Tecumseh left the camp to organize southern tribes, Harrison knew the time had come to strike. After a long, hard march, Harrison's men set up camp for the night. Before leaving, Tecumseh had warned the Prophet not to fight, but the Prophet thought God spoke to him through visions. He told the warriors that his magic would turn the white men's gunpowder into sand and their bullets soft as rain. The Indians attacked Harrison's camp at dawn.

The Indians knew Harrison rode a gray horse, and they were told to center their fire on the man riding the gray horse. When the Indians attacked, Harrison called for his horse, but it had broken its tie rope, so he rode a black horse instead. An officer riding on a light-colored horse was shot several times. Harrison remained "calm, cool and collected," according to a regular army officer. It was a close battle, but Harrison immediately sent reports that it had been a great victory. Afterward, people referred to Harrison as "Old Tip" or "Old Tippecanoe."

Harrison was made a brigadier general, and during the War of 1812, he re-captured Detroit, which had earlier been taken by the British. Chasing the British-Indian force into Canada, Harrison's army won the Battle of the Thames, in which Tecumseh was killed. There was little fighting in the West after that; Harrison resigned and returned to his farm.

In 1816, Harrison was elected to the U.S. House. He became an Ohio state senator in 1819, a member of the U.S. Senate in 1825, and minister (ambassador) to Colombia in 1828. He became a Whig for the same reason many others did; he did not like Andrew Jackson. In 1836, he received more votes for president than any other Whig. Considering the economic disasters of Van Buren's years, he was in a better position to run for president in 1840 than any of the other Whigs.

The campaign of 1840 was a long party, and everyone was invited. It featured songs, jingles, parades, barbecues, banners, and pamphlets. People, bitter over the Panic of 1837, put the blame on Van Buren, who was ridiculed unmercifully. In 1839, the Democrats reported that Harrison would be content with a barrel of hard cider, a pension of $2,000, and a chair on the front porch of his log cabin. Van Buren, on the other hand, was pictured by the Whigs as sitting in splendor sipping fine French wine. The campaign became known as the "hard cider" campaign.

The Whig campaign had a catchy phrase, "Tippecanoe and Tyler Too!" Among the words set to old songs were "The Soldiers of Tippecanoe" and the "Log Cabin Song." Even the finely-dressed Daniel Webster started wearing plain clothes when campaigning for Harrison.

Democrats were very vocal as well. They accused Harrison of heavy drinking and immorality. To them he was "Old Tip-ler." Democrats formed "O.K." clubs for "Old Kinderhook" and broke into a Whig meeting shouting, "Down with the Whigs, boys, O.K.?" At first, the term was secret, but Whigs started using it too, saying it meant, "Out of Kash" or "Out of Karacter." The Whigs then reversed it to K.O. and said that it stood for "Kicked Out!" The Whigs easily won the election. Harrison had 234 electoral votes to Van Buren's 60.

HARRISON AS PRESIDENT. Harrison's inaugural address was given outdoors on a cold, stormy day. It was the longest ever given, 105 minutes long and 8,578 words. Harrison caught a cold during that day. At the time he was elected, Harrison was 68 years old, and he felt every day of it. He agreed with Henry Clay on many things, but Harrison got tired of Clay pressuring him to appoint Clay people to high government offices. His most important appointment was Daniel Webster as secretary of state.

Harrison's common cold turned into pneumonia, and he died in April 1841. He had been president for only a month. It was said of him: "He was not a great man, but he had lived in a great time, and he had been a leader in great things."

JOHN TYLER
(1790–1862, P. 1841–1845)

Tyler was at home in Virginia when he received word that Harrison had died unexpectedly. He immediately went to Washington, D.C., and was sworn in by the chief justice of the U.S. Circuit Court at the Indian Queen Hotel. Tyler was the first vice president to become president because of death.

Tyler was born in 1790 on his family's plantation. Very little is known about his boyhood except for an incident when he was 11; he led a student revolt against a domineering teacher. He graduated from William and Mary College when he was 17 years old. Tyler became a lawyer when he was 21. He was first elected to the Virginia legislature in 1811, to the U.S. House in 1816, as governor in 1825, and to the U.S. Senate in 1827.

Tyler believed slavery was an issue for states to deal with, and the federal government could not interfere. He voted against the bill authorizing President Jackson to send federal troops to collect taxes in South Carolina. He opposed Jackson, but he disagreed with the majority of Whigs on most issues. However, the Whigs chose him for vice president in 1840 to win Southern support for the party. They had never dreamed that Tyler would be president.

TYLER AS PRESIDENT. From the beginning, Tyler had trouble establishing himself as "president," and not "acting president." At his first cabinet meeting, Webster told him that Harrison had put every decision of the cabinet to a majority vote. Tyler said that he would seek their advice, but he would never be dictated to by his cabinet. If they agreed, they were welcome to stay in the cabinet; if not, they should resign. All except Webster resigned in a few weeks.

Tyler did not support high tariffs and internal improvements paid for by the federal government. The Whigs then turned against him. When Congress passed a bill creating a new Bank of the United States, he vetoed it. That night, an angry, rock-throwing mob surrounded the White House. Tyler passed out guns to the servants, but the crowd eventually left.

In 1843, the House voted on a resolution to impeach Tyler, "vice president acting as president," for the crimes of corruption and misconduct in office. The charges were rejected by a vote of 83 in favor, 127 opposed.

Tyler's first wife was suffering from a paralytic stroke when he became president, and she died in 1842. In 1844, he fell in love with a much younger woman, and they married that year. She was a fine hostess and became well known for her entertaining.

Tyler favored annexing Texas, but many Northerners opposed admitting another slave state. When James K. Polk, who favored expansion, won the election of 1844, Congress approved annexing Texas three days before Tyler left office. Tyler returned to Virginia, where he raised a new family of seven children. In 1861, he worked to keep the peace between North and South.

When Virginia left the Union in 1861, Tyler was elected to the Confederate House of Representatives but died before he could take his seat. The U.S. government made no official announcement of his death, the only time that has been done in U.S. history. It was not until 1911 that Congress appropriated money for a monument in his honor.

Name: _____ Date: _____

Points to Ponder (W. H. Harrison, Tyler)

1. How did Harrison's opinion of slavery change? _____

_____

_____

2. How did a broken rope save Harrison's life? _____

_____

_____

3. Why did Harrison become a Whig? _____

_____

_____

4. How did Harrison's inaugural address differ from other presidents'?

_____

_____

5. Did Tyler take the position on most issues that other Whigs did?

_____

_____

6. What was unique about the announcement of Tyler's death?

_____

_____

☆ ☆ ☆ **Explore History**  ☆ ☆ ☆

1. Interview Tecumseh and his younger brother, Tenskwatawa, the Prophet. How did they differ in appearance and personality? Why was Tenskwatawa called "the Shawnee Prophet"? Which brother do you think was a better leader?

2. Write a newspaper article describing the campaign of 1840, the "hard cider" campaign. How was it different from those that had taken place before? Why was Harrison often portrayed as a simple farmer of humble birth and little education?

3. Henry Clay was never elected president; he did, however, actively participate in politics for many years. Make a time line of Henry Clay's political career.

JAMES K. POLK
(1795–1849, P. 1845–1849)

No one in 1820 could have imagined a United States extending across the continent to Oregon and California. Who could have imagined steamboats becoming common? Who could have predicted the spread of railroad lines across the mountains and prairies of America, bringing towns separated by days to cities separated by hours? In 1844, a telegraph line connected Baltimore with Washington, D.C., and it carried the message in a split second that the Democrats had chosen James K. Polk for president. The impossible was becoming more possible every day.

Polk was born in North Carolina in 1795, the son of a prosperous farmer. James's mother was very religious and raised her son in the Presbyterian Church. As a boy, he was often ill, but there was a toughness to him; his gall bladder was taken out in a surgery performed on a bare table without anesthesia. He graduated with honors from the University of North Carolina in 1818. He moved to Tennessee where he became a lawyer and a friend of Andrew Jackson. In time, he became so close to the general that Jackson was known as "Old Hickory," and Polk was known as "Young Hickory."

In 1822, Polk was elected to the Tennessee legislature, and two years later, he was elected to the U.S. House. As a loyal follower of Jackson, he was among those who gave J.Q. Adams trouble. He was faithful in attending House sessions, missing only one day in 14 years. In 1835, he was elected Speaker of the House. He left the House in 1839 to become North Carolina's governor. He was not re-elected in 1841 and failed again in 1843. He might have been washed up in politics if Van Buren had taken a firm stand favoring Texas annexation. Polk favored it, and he tied the Texas question to expansion into Oregon. The United States and Great Britain jointly controlled Oregon, but many westerners wanted the United States to claim all of Oregon. Their motto was "54-40 or fight" (54°40' is the southern boundary of Alaska, which then belonged to Russia).

At the Democratic Convention in 1844, neither Van Buren nor his opponent, Lewis Cass of Michigan, could get enough delegate support to carry them to the nomination. For the first seven ballots, no one even mentioned Polk's name. On the eighth ballot, 44 delegates voted for Polk as a compromise candidate, and on the ninth ballot, he was chosen with all 266 votes being cast for him. No one had expected it, including his Whig opponent, Henry Clay.

Clay had been a fixture in American politics for over 30 years. He was popular, had been a senator, Speaker of the House, and secretary of state. He very much wanted to be president, and he appealed to the East with his support for high tariffs and the West by favoring federal support for internal improvements. Everyone knew who Clay was, but few knew much about Polk. Clay tried to keep his support in the North by only making vague statements about accepting Texas sometime in the future.

Polk barely beat Clay with 38,000 more popular votes; in electoral votes, the majority was much greater, 275–105.

POLK AS PRESIDENT. Polk knew exactly what he wanted to accomplish. In four years, he would lower the tariff, set up an independent treasury, settle the Oregon question, and acquire California. Recent presidents had responded when Congress passed bills; he worked to get Congress to go along with his ideas. Congress reduced the tariff and created the Independent Treasury, a system used until 1913 when the Federal Reserve System was created.

There was no nonsense with him. Polk would not waste the day talking to office seekers. All appointments were made before noon. The new president was getting things done, but few people really knew him. He was like a gambler carefully playing his hand. He liked to keep people guessing, and whatever he said might or might not be what he intended to do.

Sarah Polk was much more popular than her husband, and even his worst enemies found her charming. She was very devout, however, and she allowed no card playing, wine, or dancing in the White House.

Three major problems in foreign policy were Oregon, Texas, and California. There was the possibility the United States would have to fight Great Britain and Mexico because of these issues. Polk knew that the Oregon question must be settled peacefully; then he could do whatever was necessary with Mexico.

Oregon. Some Democrats were willing to fight Great Britain for all of Oregon Country. Polk was willing to compromise by drawing the boundary at the 49° parallel of latitude (straight across from the Rocky Mountains to the Pacific Ocean). Britain wanted the region between 49° and the Columbia River and rejected the offer. When some in Congress favored war, Britain backed down, and the forty-ninth parallel became the boundary.

Texas. The Texas Revolution had taken place in 1836, and for nine years, Texas was an independent nation. Mexico claimed that Texas still belonged to them; if the United States annexed Texas, Mexico threatened war with the United States. Texans were eager to become part of the United States, and in March 1845, Congress annexed them. Polk sent a small army under General Zachary Taylor to the Rio Grande River in 1846. Mexican troops attacked them, and Polk asked Congress to declare war on Mexico.

Some Americans, including Abraham Lincoln and John C. Calhoun, opposed the war, but most rallied around the flag. The usual criticisms of the war were that the United States was bullying a weak neighbor and that this was a war to spread slavery. The war made heroes of two generals, Zachary Taylor and Winfield Scott. Taylor's victories were in northern Mexico, and Scott captured Mexico City.

California. In 1846, Americans in California revolted against Mexico (the Bear Flag Revolt) with help from John C. Frémont, who was in California with 60 armed men on a "scientific expedition." When California learned that the United States and Mexico were at war, they flew the American flag. The U.S. Navy under Robert Stockton arrived in California first, and the U.S. Army under Stephen Kearny came later. By 1848, California was safely in American hands.

Gaining all of this land caused great discussion about whether the area would be open to slavery. In 1846, Congress debated the Wilmot Proviso, which said that all lands taken from Mexico would be closed to slavery. It passed in the House, but was defeated in the Senate. The Proviso was still much on people's minds when Polk left office.

Polk was very happy to leave the presidency. He wrote: "I shall be a happier man in my retirement than I have been during the four years I have filled the highest office in the gift of my countrymen." After Zachary Taylor took office, Polk and his wife moved back to Tennessee. He died in 1849.

Name: _____ Date: _____

Points to Ponder (Polk)

1. A mentor is a teacher who helps someone with his or her career. Who was Polk's mentor?

   _____

2. If a person favored 54-40 or fight, what part of North America were they interested in?

   _____

   _____

3. A "dark horse" is a candidate who unexpectedly wins a nomination. Was Polk a "dark horse"? Why or why not?

   _____

   _____

   _____

   _____

4. Why did some Americans oppose the Mexican War?

   _____

   _____

   _____

   _____

5. Would you consider Polk a great president? Why or why not?

   _____

   _____

   _____

   _____

☆ ☆ ☆ **Explore History**  ☆ ☆ ☆

1. Make a map or time line of the annexation of states during this period.

2. Write a short biography on John C. Frémont or Winfield Scott.

3. If you opposed slavery, would you favor the Wilmot Proviso? Debate with members of your class why or why not.

ZACHARY TAYLOR
(1784–1850, P. 1849–1850)

Zachary Taylor was an old soldier who never considered running for president until he became angry with President Polk. If the Whigs wanted him to run, he was willing. Once again, the nation had a folksy man of the people as their president.

Taylor was born into a large and wealthy Virginia family. In 1785, the family moved to Kentucky in an area with no schools and no teachers. There was only work, and the stories told by his father who had served in the Revolution. In 1808, Taylor was commissioned as a first lieutenant in the army. In 1810, he was made a captain and married Margaret Smith in a log cabin. She was the daughter of a planter whose father had been a major in the Continental Army. Margaret went wherever Zachary was stationed and never complained about the crude accommodations provided at army forts. Their daughter later married Jefferson Davis, a young officer, but she died only three months later. Davis in time became president of the Confederacy, and one of Taylor's sons became a Confederate general.

Taylor served in several Indian campaigns including the Black Hawk War and a Florida campaign against the Seminoles. In 1841, he became commander of the western division of the army, with headquarters at Fort Smith, Arkansas. In 1844, he was moved to Louisiana, and promoted to brevet (temporary) brigadier general.

By that time, Taylor was legendary for his manner of dressing. He was usually dressed like a simple farmer in a straw hat and baggy pants, and young officers first reporting for duty had no idea he was their commanding officer. Winfield Scott, always well-dressed in a splendid uniform, had the nickname of "Old Fuss and Feathers." Taylor's nickname was "Old Rough and Ready." He slept in simple tents and ate simple foods, and his men loved and respected him.

In 1846, his army was ordered to the Rio Grande River by President Polk. A patrol was attacked, and some of his men were killed. Taylor sent the message to Washington, and Polk used it to convince Congress that "American blood had been shed on American soil." Before war was declared, two more battles were fought, Palo Alto and Resaca de la Palma. Both battles were victories for the United States, and some were looking at Taylor as a future presidential candidate. Since he had never voted, no one knew whether he was Whig or Democrat. Polk suspected he was a Whig, so he formed a new army under Winfield Scott, taking men from Taylor's army.

At Monterrey, Taylor's advancing army defeated a much larger Mexican force. Running short on supplies, Taylor allowed the Mexicans to leave with their arms. Polk was furious, and ordered him not to advance any further. Taking advantage of the opportunity to attack a smaller American force, the Mexicans gathered a large army of 14,000 men against Taylor's army of 5,000 at Buena Vista. While Taylor's army held its position, the Mexicans retreated with heavy casualties.

Taylor was a hero to the nation but was criticized by Polk for advancing his army. Taylor informed the Whigs that if they nominated him, he would accept. The letter informing Taylor he had been chosen came with postage due, so he refused to accept it. A few weeks later, another letter arrived from the Whigs, notifying him that he was the nominee.

In 1848, there were three candidates in the field: Taylor (Whig), Lewis Cass (Democrat), and Martin Van Buren (Free Soil). There was the usual mudslinging. Taylor was compared to a Caesar or Napoleon, who would create wars for his military glory. They described Mrs. Taylor as a poor, illiterate woman who smoked a corncob pipe. In truth, Mrs. Taylor was allergic to the smell of tobacco smoke, and her husband had given up smoking for that reason. The Whigs said Cass was a sly politician who had sold whites into slavery. Facts disturbed neither side.

The Free Soilers chose Van Buren only three months before the election. They opposed slavery expanding into the territories. Van Buren did not carry any states, but did get 291,000 votes. Free Soil influence was going to grow stronger in the North in the next few years.

Taylor won the election with 1.36 million popular votes to Cass's 1.22 million votes. The electoral vote was 163–127.

TAYLOR AS PRESIDENT. Since he had no political experience and was not well-informed on many issues, Taylor needed someone to guide him. Instead of turning to Henry Clay (the party leader) or a Southern leader like John C. Calhoun, he chose William Seward of New York to help him. Most of the cabinet opposed slavery expansion into territories. Even though he was a Southerner and slave owner himself, Taylor came out in favor of making California and New Mexico free states. The South was angry, and many Southern Whigs left the party. In Congress, there were heated debates over slavery, and Southern members talked about secession (leaving the Union).

Henry Clay returned to the Senate in 1849 and began to work with others on a compromise between the North and South. He put together what came to be known as the Compromise of 1850. Its five main parts were: (1) California was to be admitted as a free state; (2) a territorial government was to be organized in New Mexico and Utah; (3) the Texas-New Mexico boundary was to be settled in favor of New Mexico with Texas to receive $10 million; (4) the slave trade was to be ended in Washington, D.C.; and (5) a stronger fugitive slave law was to be put into effect. Taylor did not support the Compromise; he stayed with his original idea of forming states in California and New Mexico. His views were ignored as Congress debated the issues Clay had proposed.

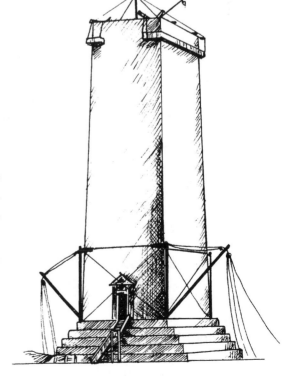

On July 4, 1850, Taylor presided at the laying of the cornerstone for the Washington Monument. After the ceremony, he suffered a stroke and died on July 9. After the funeral, Mrs. Taylor left Washington and never returned. She lived the rest of her life in a small home in Louisiana.

MILLARD FILLMORE
(1800–1874, P. 1850–1853)

For the second time, a vice president became president because of death. The public knew even less about Fillmore than they had known about Tyler. After he left office, the public quickly forgot him.

Millard was born in a log cabin in New York state, the son of poor farmers. Millard received very little schooling, but he was bright, and at 18 became a clerk at a lawyer's office. A year later, he became a lawyer. He married when he was 26. People saw in him the potential for a politician. He had been born in a log cabin, was good-looking, honest, and made friends easily. He joined the Anti-Masonic party, a group opposed to secret organizations. In 1828, he was elected to the New York legislature, where he proposed a law that would end imprisonment for debt. In 1831, he was elected to the U.S. House; he later became a Whig when that party was formed.

After he became chairman of the House Committee on Ways and Means, he wrote the tariff in 1842, which raised taxes on imported manufactured goods. He left the House in 1844, ran for governor, and lost. Fillmore became chancellor of the University of Buffalo in 1846. In 1848, the Whigs chose him for vice president, and in 1850, he became president.

FILLMORE AS PRESIDENT. Personally, Fillmore opposed slavery, but he feared a national disaster if the South was not satisfied. His whole cabinet resigned the day he took office; he asked them to stay for at least a month, but they stayed only one week. The people he appointed all favored the Compromise of 1850. As the different portions of the Compromise passed, he signed them. The North was quite angry with the new fugitive slave law, but Fillmore was determined to enforce it.

The West was growing rapidly, and it became clear that a railroad to the Pacific would help it grow even faster. Fillmore worked with Senator Stephen Douglas to get grants for railroad construction. A strip across northern Mexico was bought for $10 million (the Gadsden Purchase) for the purpose of gaining the right of way for a southern railroad route.

Western Indian tribes gathered at Fort Laramie in 1851. Each tribe was given a large area of land, where they were promised that they could live for all time. The government did not keep its word, and these areas became smaller as more settlers moved into the region.

In 1852, Commodore Matthew Perry sailed to Japan in an effort to open trade with that isolated nation. The fleet arrived in January 1853. An agreement was not signed until 1854. Even though the agreement was only to help shipwrecked sailors, it was the first crack in the door to trade between the United States and Japan; few realized its importance at the time.

When the Whig Convention met in 1852, the party passed over Fillmore and chose Winfield Scott as its nominee. He was defeated by Franklin Pierce, who became president in 1853. Mrs. Fillmore died a few weeks after her husband left office. No more Whigs were ever elected president. In 1856, Fillmore ran for president on a combined Whig/Know-Nothing ticket (the Know-Nothings were against Catholics and immigrants). In that election, Fillmore carried only Maryland.

During the Civil War, Fillmore was critical of Lincoln and supported his Democratic opponent, George McClellan, in 1864. After McClellan's defeat, Fillmore never ventured into public life again. He died in 1874.

Name: _____ Date: _____

Points to Ponder (Taylor, Fillmore)

1. What nickname was given to Taylor? Why was it given?

   _____

   _____

   _____

2. What policy did Free Soilers want? Who ran on the Free Soil ticket in 1848?

   _____

   _____

   _____

3. What two parts of the Compromise of 1850 appealed most to Northerners?

   _____

   _____

   _____

   What part appealed most to Southerners? _____

   _____

   _____

4. Who opened trade with Japan? What was included in the agreement he made? Why was this important?

   _____

   _____

   _____

5. What candidate and party did Fillmore support in the 1864 election?

   _____

 Explore History

1. Make a model or drawing of the Washington Monument.

2. Write a newspaper article about the Gadsden Purchase and the building of the railroad.

3. Make a map of land given to the different Indian tribes at this time.

FRANKLIN PIERCE
(1804–1869, P. 1853–1857)

At the 1852 convention, the Democrats were deadlocked. No candidate could get the two-thirds majority the party rules dictated. On the 35th ballot, Virginia cast 15 votes for Franklin Pierce; he received 55 votes on the 48th ballot. Then there was a rush to support him, and on the 49th ballot, Pierce was chosen. Again, people were asking who this man was, and as had happened in the case of Polk, they discovered he was the next president.

Pierce was born to be a politician. His father had been a general in the Revolution and later became governor of New Hampshire. Franklin graduated from Bowdoin College, became a lawyer at 22, a member of the state legislature at 24, speaker of the state house at 26, a member of the U.S. House at 28, and a senator at 32. He was well liked and charming, but spent too much time drinking with his fellow politicians. He was very agreeable and tried to please everyone. In 1842, he resigned from the Senate at his wife's request. She hated politics and wanted Franklin to drop out of politics. In 1846, President Polk tried to tempt him with the job of attorney general, but he turned it down.

In 1847, Pierce enlisted as a private to fight in the Mexican War. He was elected colonel of his regiment in February and was a brigadier general in March. He was in several battles, but as Whigs later pointed out, his record was not impressive. He resigned from the army in 1848. When he returned home, he turned down a Senate seat offered him by the governor. When some supporters urged him to try for the Democratic presidential nomination, his wife was not happy about it, and he promised her that he would not seek the job. When he was chosen to be the nominee on the forty-ninth ballot, she accepted it as God's will.

The campaign of 1852 centered on the qualities of the two candidates rather than their programs. The Whig candidate, Winfield Scott, had served his country well since the War of 1812. His victories in the Mexican War had forced Mexico to make peace. However, his reputation as "Old Fuss and Feathers" was also well known. He loved parades and fancy dress uniforms. Scott was a general, but clearly he was not cut from the same cloth as Washington, Jackson, Harrison, and Taylor had been.

Pierce's record in the Mexican War was soon being ridiculed by the Whigs, who charged he had fainted in two battles, had become ill and gone to bed during the third, and had missed the fourth by an hour. They put out a book entitled "The Military Services of General Pierce" that was an inch high and a half-inch wide. They also criticized his drinking. The Whigs said he was "the hero of many a well-fought bottle."

In the election, Pierce carried 27 states and received 254 electoral votes. Scott had only carried four states and received 42 electoral votes. The Whigs would try to keep their party alive, but this was their last full-scale campaign for president.

Just before he became president, a tragedy occurred that devastated Pierce and his wife. They had three sons, but two had died before they were four years old. The third son, Bennie, was accidentally killed in front of his shocked parents when a railroad car ran over him. Mrs. Pierce never fully recovered, and President Pierce began his term deeply depressed.

PIERCE AS PRESIDENT. The slavery issue made the work of Congress difficult. The split over who would be Speaker of the House tied up the representatives' time for nearly two months. It was not until the 133rd ballot that they chose Nathaniel Banks of Massachusetts as Speaker.

For the cabinet, Pierce chose only pro-slavery members. Among them was Jefferson Davis from Mississippi as secretary of war. Davis tried an unusual experiment. In 1855, Congress voted $30,000 to buy camels in Africa to haul supplies across the desert Southwest. Camel drivers were brought in to work them. The experiment had hardly started before the new secretary of war canceled it in 1857. After keeping the animals a while, they were sold in 1864; some were used in circuses, and others roamed freely. Reports of camel sightings were heard for many years afterward.

Every unemployed or ambitious Democrat in the country applied for a government job; only about one in ten got one. This made one person happy and nine angry. Pierce wasted much of his time dealing with office seekers. People wondered if he was up to the task of being president.

In 1854, Senator Stephen Douglas of Illinois proposed the Kansas-Nebraska bill. It would create the territories of Kansas and Nebraska and would let the people there decide whether to have slavery. The possibility that slavery might come into the region north of the Missouri Compromise line of 36°30′ outraged many Northerners. Pierce supported it, and the bill was finally passed. In Kansas, pro-slave and anti-slave settlers clashed in battles and earned the territory the nickname of "Bleeding Kansas."

As the result of political arguing, the Republican Party was formed in 1854. Its members were mostly old Whigs, Free Soilers, and anti-slavery people; they were nearly all in free states. The South feared the Republicans were going to free the slaves. The Know-Nothing party became much stronger during this time. They were members of a secret organization, and if asked about it, they were to reply: "I know nothing." They were against Catholics and immigrants and were organized in both the North and South.

In 1856, Pierce wanted to be re-elected but could not even get the Democratic nomination. After Buchanan was elected, the Pierces went to Europe for nearly two years. When he returned, some people wanted Pierce to run again, but he refused. During the Civil War, he opposed Lincoln's policies and called the war "fearful, fruitless, fatal," on the day the Battle of Gettysburg was won. This ruined what little of his reputation had survived his years in the White House. Pierce died in 1869.

JAMES BUCHANAN
(1791–1868, P. 1857–1861)

Few presidents ever came into office when there was more tension in the air. Congress was not only divided between Democrats and Republicans, but between Northerners and Southerners. Each side blamed the other for the bloodshed in Kansas. Many members of Congress came to the sessions armed after the 1856 caning of Senator Charles Sumner by Preston Brooks in the Senate chamber. Nine days after that occurred, Democrats met for their national convention in Cincinnati. The party looked for someone who was "available" (meaning he could win the election). The person they chose had been in England during the troubles of recent years, so no one could blame him for anything.

Buchanan was born in a log cabin in western Pennsylvania in 1791. His father had come from Ireland in 1783, married an American woman, and ran a country store. James learned arithmetic keeping records at the store, and he studied Latin and Greek with a local minister. He graduated from Dickinson College in 1809 and studied law in Lancaster. He became a successful lawyer and was worth $300,000 when he became president.

During the War of 1812, he enlisted as a private to defend Ft. McHenry from the British attack. He served in the Pennsylvania legislature from 1814 to 1816. He fell in love with Ann Coleman, and they were engaged in 1819. They got into an argument, and she went to Philadelphia to stay with a sister; she soon died, and it was rumored that she had committed suicide. Buchanan never married.

Buchanan was elected to the House of Representatives in 1820. At first he was a Federalist, but he switched parties in 1824, and supported Jackson against John Q. Adams. In 1831, President Jackson chose him as minister to Russia. He did not enjoy life there but succeeded in making the first trade agreement with the Russian czar. He returned home in 1833. Pennsylvania chose him as a senator in 1834, and he stayed until 1845. Buchanan then served as President Polk's secretary of state and then as Pierce's minister to Great Britain.

The new Republican Party met for the first time in 1856. They chose the famed explorer John C. Frémont as their candidate. Frémont had no political experience and was impulsive and self-centered, but he was rich enough to pay his campaign expenses. Frémont opposed slavery's expansion into the territories and wanted to build a railroad to California. Many Democrats feared war would come if Frémont was elected. They said the South would secede (leave the Union). The Republicans argued that the South had threatened to secede many times before, but never had.

The Know-Nothings joined what was left of the Whig party in nominating Fillmore for President.

When Buchanan returned home in 1856, the Democrats chose him as their presidential candidate with John C. Breckinridge from Kentucky as vice president. With many Southern friends, Buchanan found a much broader group to support him than any of the other candidates.

In the election, Buchanan carried 19 states with 174 electoral votes, Frémont won in 11 states with 114 electoral votes, and Fillmore carried one state with eight electoral votes. The Democrats controlled both houses of Congress.

Buchanan had great hopes for his administration, but he knew there were others more intent on tearing the nation apart than holding it together. At first, he blamed the abolitionists for being the troublemakers creating fear in the South.

One of those was Harriet Beecher Stowe, whose book *Uncle Tom's Cabin* had become a best seller. It told the story of good, simple slaves in the hands of an evil master, Simon Legree. Her book had sold 300,000 copies in its first year, and brought tears to many eyes in the United States, Great Britain, and other nations. Another abolitionist was Reverend Henry Ward Beecher, who said that anti-slavery settlers in Kansas needed rifles, not Bibles, and started collecting money for guns. There were abolitionist writers like William Lloyd Garrison, whose newspaper, the *Liberator,* attacked slave owners in every issue. Some abolitionists were involved in the Underground Railroad, sneaking fugitive slaves out of the South and taking them to Canada.

BUCHANAN AS PRESIDENT. Buchanan hoped that history would say he was a good and kindly man who held the nation together. Instead, when he left office he was seen as weak, incompetent, and a total failure.

His troubles began when the Supreme Court handed down its decision in *Dred Scott v. Sandford.* The majority of the Court ruled that blacks were not citizens and could not bring cases to the federal courts. In addition, the Court said the Missouri Compromise was unconstitutional. Southerners were delighted, because the decision meant they could spread slavery into the territories. Many Northerners were furious, and the Court's prestige dropped rapidly.

Kansans had chosen a pro-slavery legislature, which Northern settlers ignored, and Free Soilers had chosen an anti-slavery legislature, which Southern settlers opposed. Buchanan sided with the pro-slavery legislature even though it was unfairly chosen. Senator Stephen Douglas split with Buchanan over this, and many other Democrats agreed with Douglas.

In 1858, Senator Douglas's term expired, and he ran for re-election against Abraham Lincoln. Buchanan supporters in Illinois worked against Douglas, making his campaign harder. After campaigning separately for a time, Lincoln and Douglas held seven debates in the state of Illinois. At Freeport, Douglas said the people could stop slavery from coming in by not protecting it. This made the South angry with Douglas.

John Brown, who had helped cause trouble in Kansas, was in the headlines again in 1859. He and a group of followers planned to stir up a slave uprising by attacking the federal armory at Harper's Ferry, Virginia. After they had taken over the town, federal troops led by Colonel Robert E. Lee arrived and surrounded Brown's men, who surrendered after a fight. They were found guilty of treason against Virginia and were hanged.

In 1860, the Democrats split, with Northern Democrats backing Douglas, and Southern Democrats backing John Breckinridge of Kentucky. The Republicans chose Lincoln for president. A new party formed in the border states (those close to the North, but where slavery was legal), called the Constitutional Union party; their candidate was John Bell.

After Lincoln won the election, South Carolina seceded in December 1860 and six other states followed before Buchanan left office in March. All efforts to settle the differences had failed. Buchanan argued that they could not leave the Union, but he did not have the power to make them stay. When his term was up, Buchanan returned home to Lancaster, Pennsylvania. He died there in 1868.

Name: _____ Date: _____

Points to Ponder (Pierce, Buchanan)

1. What was the Whigs' opinion of Pierce's record during the Mexican War?

   _____

   _____

   _____

2. What tragedy affected Pierce's life in the White House?

   _____

   _____

3. Why did his party refuse to consider Pierce for a second term?

   _____

   _____

   _____

4. Who did Buchanan blame for the troubles between the North and South?

   _____

   _____

   Who were three of these "troublemakers"? _____

   _____

   _____

5. What happened after the election of 1860 that showed how the South felt about Lincoln?

   _____

   _____

   _____

 **Explore History**

1. Write a mini-report on camels.

2. Read *Uncle Tom's Cabin*, by Harriet Beecher Stowe. Give a book report on it.

3. As a class, research the Underground Railroad. Was there a stop on the Underground Railroad in your town or in a town near you? Have a class discussion on the outcome of your research.

ABRAHAM LINCOLN
(1809–1865, P. 1861–1865)

Four score and seven years ago our fathers brought forth upon this continent, a new nation.

In the view of many Americans today, Abraham Lincoln was the greatest president of all. He is a symbol of democracy, the common man who rises to the top. Young people admire him for leading the nation during the Civil War and freeing the slaves. He fought a bitter war but never became bitter. Many feel closer to him than any other president; he was a man with little education who worked hard, made wise statements, was a friend to the common man, and was killed when he was most needed. Modern Americans may be surprised to find that people of his time did not have such a high opinion of Lincoln, and he was often ridiculed in the press.

Most of Lincoln's time and effort was spent on winning the Civil War, but out of this time also came changes that affected the future: chartering of railroads to the Pacific, homesteads for farmers in the West, and land set aside for colleges to teach agriculture and mechanics.

Lincoln was born in a log cabin in Kentucky. His father, Tom, was a hardworking man with no education. Abraham's mother, Nancy Hanks, came from a poor Virginia family. Tom moved the family to Indiana in 1816. Nancy died in 1818. Tom then married Mrs. Sarah Johnston in 1819. Mrs. Johnston and her three children moved in with the Lincolns. She was a good stepmother to Abraham, and he appreciated her.

The opportunity for an education was very limited, but Abraham learned to read and borrowed books whenever he could. The Bible was probably the only book the family owned, and he read it constantly. As president, he often quoted it from memory. Most of his time was spent in hard work. Lincoln was thin but strong; the ax and plow were often the companions of his youth.

In 1830, the Lincolns moved to Illinois. Abraham helped Tom put in their first crop, then took a job as a country store clerk at New Salem. The residents of New Salem were very helpful to the young bachelor. The women gave him meals, and one of the men introduced him to the works of Shakespeare and the poet Robert Burns. When the store failed, Lincoln joined the militia and was elected captain during the Black Hawk War. He was in no battles but "fought a good many bloody struggles with the mosquitoes." He bought a store with a partner; the store lost money, and his share of the debt when the store closed was $1,000. It took years to pay off the debt, but, by doing so, he earned the nickname of "Honest Abe."

Lincoln ran for the Illinois state legislature in 1834 on the Whig ticket, and he won re-election three times. By his second term, he was Whig leader of the state House of Representatives. In 1837, he and another member, Dan Stone, wrote their opinions of slavery. They admitted it was legal in the slave states, but it was "both injustice and bad policy."

In 1834, Lincoln also began studying law, sometimes walking 20 miles to Springfield to borrow books. He became a lawyer in 1836 and moved to the state capital. After working as junior partner with two outstanding lawyers, he joined William Herndon in the partnership that lasted the rest of Lincoln's life. He was very thorough in preparing his cases; he could charm an uneducated jury with simple explanations and witty remarks or a well-educated judge with his knowledge of the law.

Lincoln married Mary Todd in 1842 after a two-year courtship. She was lively, intelligent, ambitious, and temperamental. Their marriage was not smooth, and rumors spread that Lincoln was very unhappy with her. Most of the stories were not true, but untrue gossip about her being pro-Southern during the Civil War hurt his reputation. Of their four sons, only one lived to be an adult.

In 1846, Lincoln was elected to the U.S. House of Representatives, where he made himself unpopular by opposing the Mexican War. Lincoln knew he could not win another term, so he returned to practicing law. His clients now were often large corporations, and he became prosperous.

It was not until 1858 that Lincoln returned to politics. Like many others, he opposed the Kansas-Nebraska Act that Senator Stephen Douglas of Illinois had pushed through. Lincoln still believed slavery was wrong, but Douglas said it was legal and nothing should be done about it. Lincoln was so successful in his attacks that he was soon leader of the opponents of Douglas during the Senate campaign. The debates between Lincoln and Douglas were reported across the nation, making Lincoln famous. Douglas was successful in winning his Senate seat again, but Lincoln's reputation made him a contender for the Republican presidential nomination in 1860.

Lincoln was opposed by William Seward, Salmon Chase, and several native son candidates (those supported only by their state delegations). Lincoln defeated them in a noisy convention held in Chicago. In the national election, he won a majority of electoral votes, all from Northern states. As soon as his victory was announced, South Carolina prepared to secede from the Union. Between December 1860 and March 1861 when Lincoln became president, seven states left the Union.

LINCOLN AS PRESIDENT. In his inaugural address, Lincoln said that the choice of whether to make war or not was up to the Southern states. He, however, had no choice in whether to defend "property and places" belonging to the federal government. Fort Sumter, in the harbor of Charleston, South Carolina, became the spot where the issue of defending "property and places" was focused. The commander at the fort, Major Robert Anderson, was running short of supplies and would have to surrender unless more were sent. Instead of sending more troops, Lincoln informed the governor of South Carolina he was sending supplies. When Anderson refused to surrender the fort, Confederate guns opened fire. That was the beginning of the Civil War.

Lincoln and the war (1861–1863). To build up the army, Lincoln called on the governors to supply 75,000 men. In four slave states (Virginia, North Carolina, Tennessee, and Arkansas), the states left the Union rather than fight their Southern friends. In four slave-holding border states (Missouri, Kentucky, Maryland, and Delaware), pro-Southern sentiment was not strong enough to pull the state from the Union. Military leaders had to make up their minds whether to fight for the North or South. The most important officer to leave the Northern army was Colonel Robert E. Lee.

At the beginning of the war, the Confederates won most battles. At First Bull Run, General Irwin McDowell's army ran from the field. In the Peninsular campaign, General George McClellan's army came close to the Confederate capital of Richmond, but was forced to withdraw by troops now led by General Lee. General John Pope replaced McClellan, but he was defeated at Second Bull Run. Lincoln chose McClellan again, but McClellan did not pursue the Confederates after the battle at Antietam, and he was fired again. The new general replacing McClellan was Ambrose Burnside, who suffered terrible losses in his blundering attack at Fredericksburg.

In the West, the war was going better for the Union. General Ulysses Grant won two small victories at Forts Henry and Donelson, and a major victory at Shiloh, all in Tennessee.

Lincoln knew little about strategy at first, but was a quick learner and became much wiser about military affairs by the end of the war. An important change that occurred during the war was in the navies. The North tried to blockade Southern ports at the beginning of the war, and the South started using blockade runners, sleek ships built close to the water. To attack the large wooden ships of the Union fleet, the South began building ironclads, old wooden ships with iron plates to protect them. One of these was the old *Merrimack,* renamed the *Virginia.* To protect the Union fleet, a strange new type of ship, the *Monitor,* was built. The two ships fought it out in Hampton Roads. Neither ship fought again. The Union navy built more *Monitors* and used them to get control of rivers and ports. The Confederates built a submarine, the *Hunley,* but when it sank while attacking a Union naval ship, it was not replaced.

Lincoln and slavery. During the early days of the war, as much as Lincoln disliked slavery, he resisted pressure to end it. There were two major problems: (1) the border states might become so angry they would leave the Union; and (2) the Constitution says that private property (including slaves) cannot be taken without just compensation. The government would have to buy them, and many in Congress opposed doing that. Lincoln tried to persuade border states to agree to a price of $400 per slave to be paid to loyal owners; they turned him down.

Some of the Union generals in 1861 and early 1862 began issuing orders that slaves of disloyal masters were to be freed, and Lincoln canceled the orders. By the summer of 1862, he began to change his mind. There were several reasons: (1) foreign nations did not like slavery, and he could get much more cooperation from them if he freed slaves; (2) the Union army had lost thousands of men; they could be replaced by black troops; (3) many in the North had changed their minds about slavery and now wanted it ended; and (4) the South would have a harder time controlling slaves if the slaves knew they would be free when they escaped to Union lines.

After the battle at Antietam in September 1862, Lincoln issued the preliminary Emancipation Proclamation. It announced that slaves in those areas in Confederate hands would be freed on January 1, 1863. On New Year's Day 1863, the Emancipation Proclamation listed those areas where slaves were to be freed. The Proclamation did not apply to areas in Union hands, so it only affected a few slaves at first. As the Union army advanced, slaves began leaving the farms and plantations of the South, following Union troops. It was not until the Thirteenth Amendment was ratified in 1865, however, that slavery came to an end in every American state and territory.

The turning point in the war. In July 1863, two major struggles were going on at the same time. In the West, General Grant's army was slowly tightening the grip on Vicksburg, Mississippi. This was important because Vicksburg was the last remaining crossing place on the Mississippi River between the western Confederate states and those in the east. At the same time, Lee's army was met at Gettysburg, Pennsylvania, in a struggle lasting from July 1st to July 4th. Lee was defeated, and his army retreated back to the South. In November, a cemetery at the battle site was ready for dedication, and Lincoln then gave the Gettysburg Address. Lincoln gave very few speeches as president, and that made this one special. In it, he said the war was being fought "so that government of the people, by the people, and for the people shall not perish from the earth."

Lincoln put Grant in command of all Union armies. Grant put General William T. Sherman in charge in the West, and he took field command of the army in the East. Under Grant, casualties went up. Many blamed Lincoln for the heavy losses in the war, but Lincoln stood by Grant because he was a fighter.

The election of 1864. With a presidential election coming up, Lincoln felt he needed Democratic support to win. He picked a Tennessee Democrat, Andrew Johnson, for vice president. The Democrats chose General George McClellan for president. Lincoln worried that he might not get re-elected at first, but good news from the war helped. David Farragut won a naval battle at Mobile Bay in August, and Sherman reached Atlanta in September. Lincoln won the election, 212–21 in electoral votes and by over 400,000 popular votes.

The second inaugural address was unusual in a nation that had been in bitter warfare for three years. Lincoln wanted the nation to unite in spirit, and asked for "malice toward none" and "charity for all."

War's end. Many men died in the last phase of the war, and Lee's troops put up brave defenses in the battles of the Wilderness, Spotsylvania, Cold Harbor, and Petersburg. Sherman's army reached Savannah, Georgia, on December 20, 1864, and they then marched north through the Carolinas. Lee retreated in April and was cornered at Appomattox Courthouse, where he surrendered on April 9.

News of Lee's surrender thrilled most Northerners, but it disturbed John Wilkes Booth, a famous actor who supported the Southern cause. He shot Lincoln at Ford's Theater on the evening of April 14; Lincoln died the next day.

Name: _____ Date: _____

Points to Ponder (Lincoln)

1. How much education did Lincoln have? What was his most-read book?

   _____

   _____

2. How did he get the nickname of "Honest Abe"? _____

   _____

   _____

3. What caused Lincoln to serve in the U.S. House only one term?

   _____

   _____

   _____

4. What happened when Lincoln tried to send supplies to Fort Sumter?

   _____

   _____

   _____

5. What two battles helped Lincoln's chances of being re-elected in 1864?

   _____

6. What important event occurred April 9, 1865? _____

   _____

   On April 14, 1865? Who was involved? _____

   _____

   _____

 **Explore History**

1. Stage a mock debate about slavery, such as Lincoln and Douglas may have had.

2. Draw a sketch of an ironclad or the submarine, the *Hunley*.

3. Make a map or make a time line of the battles won and lost by the North and South.

4. Have each member of the class select a famous person who was active during the Civil War and act him or her out in front of the class. Some suggestions are Sojourner Truth, Harriet Tubman, Stephen Foster, Mathew Brady, or General George McClellan.

ANDREW JOHNSON

(1808–1875, P. 1865–1869)

No other man ever became president under the unusual circumstances Johnson did. Not only was he replacing an assassinated president, but the nation was divided by war, politics, sections of the country, and critical issues. Johnson took strong stands on issues, which resulted in his impeachment and near-removal from office. He was brave and stubborn and refused to compromise.

Johnson was born in North Carolina, the son of tavern workers; his father died when he was three years old. Andrew's mother took in washing and sewing to support the family. She apprenticed him to a tailor when he was 14 years old; he was treated badly and ran away two years later. He moved to Tennessee. When he was 18 years old, he married Eliza McCardle, who was 16. There is some question about whether he could read and write before they married, but she encouraged him to study; his favorite topics were the Constitution and Andrew Jackson.

Johnson's small tailor shop in Greeneville, Tennessee, became a place for men to discuss politics. He worked his way up as an elected official from alderman to mayor to both houses of the state legislature. In 1843, he was elected to the U.S. House. Even though he was a slave owner, he did not always vote with Southerners in Congress. He voted for annexing Texas, but he favored admitting California and Oregon as free states. He was more concerned with helping the poor farmer than rich slave owner, and he wanted a homestead law giving land to poor whites.

In 1851, Johnson became governor of Tennessee and supported laws for free public schools and opposed renting out convicts as laborers. When giving speeches, he sometimes faced hostile crowds but never changed his topic to make them happy with him. He was chosen for the U.S. Senate in 1857 and pushed for homesteads as he had done before. In 1862, the Homestead Act was finally passed. On the hot topic of the time, slavery, he supported the right of a person to own slaves, but he opposed Southerners who wanted to secede. In 1860, he supported John C. Breckinridge for president.

When Southern congressmen gave up their seats after Lincoln was elected, Johnson denounced secession as treason. On his way back to Tennessee to oppose its secession, he was roughed up by crowds gathered at railroad stations along the way. He stubbornly spoke out against secession back home and had to escape to Kentucky to avoid arrest when Tennessee seceded. He was the only Southern congressman who did not resign his seat in the Union government. His devotion to the Union impressed Lincoln.

After the Union army had cleared Confederates out of part of Tennessee, Lincoln appointed Johnson as military governor with the rank of brigadier general. He performed his job honestly and was important in bringing loyal civilian government to the state.

In 1864, the Republicans and War Democrats united in the National Union Party ticket. Lincoln chose Johnson to be vice president in the hope it would draw Democrats and border staters to the ticket. Johnson was never asked to change parties, and he remained a Democrat at heart.

Vice presidency. An embarrassing event marred Johnson's reputation. He had typhoid fever before he was inaugurated, and a senator gave him a flask of whiskey to drink. When he entered the hot Senate chamber and gave a short speech, the liquor went to his head, and he was obviously intoxicated. Six weeks later, Johnson was president.

JOHNSON AS PRESIDENT. The first few weeks after Johnson came into office, attention focused on ending the war and punishing those involved in the Lincoln assassination. Johnson had little trouble from Democrats, but it did not take long for him to begin having trouble with radical Republicans who wanted the rebels punished and the freed slaves to be given the vote. Johnson gave many pardons to Southerners who requested them as he carried out the policies he believed Lincoln had wanted.

Johnson believed Southern states should be restored quickly, with only those leaders of the rebellion excluded. States began creating governments that regulated freed slaves with Black Codes. Some parts of these codes were necessary: marriages and responsibilities as parents, for example. Others made the blacks inferior: vagrancy laws that made them work, contract laws the illiterate former slaves could not understand, and laws that kept them from entering certain occupations. Radicals charged that the South was trying to bring slavery back in a new form.

Johnson believed in a strong presidency and felt he should run the Reconstruction of the South. Congressional Republicans felt they should be in charge now that the war was over. Johnson opposed the Freedmen's Bureau Bill that provided aid to blacks. He said that providing relief, education, and medical care were state responsibilities, not federal. He opposed the Fourteenth Amendment, which made blacks citizens of the United States.

Radical Republicans were determined that the South would not be allowed to run its affairs until it showed the proper respect for Congress, the freedmen, and the Republican Party. Generals became military governors, and Freedmen's Bureau courts settled labor disputes. Those elected to Congress from Southern states were refused their seats.

Congress started limiting Johnson's powers, including the right to remove officeholders without the consent of the Senate. When Johnson vetoed this "Tenure of Office" bill, Congress overrode the veto. When Johnson tried to fire Secretary of War Stanton, the radicals in Congress used the law to impeach Johnson. After the House voted to impeach him, the Senate held the trial to remove him from office. Johnson escaped being removed from office by one vote.

Johnson's great achievement in foreign policy was buying Alaska from Russia for $7.2 million.

In 1875, Johnson returned to the Senate, once again representing Tennessee. He received strong applause, but his stay was brief. He died later in the year.

ULYSSES S. GRANT
(1822–1885, P. 1869–1877)

When the Civil War ended, the most popular hero of the North was General Ulysses Grant. He had risen from obscurity to fame in less than four years, another example of the average American who had become a success. However, his reputation was not helped by his years as president, because scandals were much too common.

Grant was born in Ohio and named Hiram Ulysses Grant. Schools were available, and he received a good education for that time. He worked as a farmhand and helped in his father's tannery. In 1839, his father learned there was an opening at West Point; Hiram did not want to go, but he obeyed his father. Upon arriving, he learned that his Congressman had turned in his name as Ulysses Simpson Grant. He preferred that to the initials "H.U.G.," and from then on was "U.S. Grant." His only successes at West Point were expert horseback riding and graduating. After graduating in 1843, he was appointed a brevet (temporary) second lieutenant in infantry. He was stationed outside St. Louis and met Julia Dent, whom he later married in 1848.

Grant disapproved of the Mexican War, but he fought under Taylor and Scott in many battles. By war's end, he was a brevet captain. After the war, he was stationed at New York for a while, then he was sent to the Pacific Northwest where he began drinking. His commanding officer did not like him, and when he found Grant drunk, told him to resign or face court martial. Grant resigned to avoid hurting Julia's reputation.

Grant's life was going nowhere now. He tried farming outside St. Louis, but failed. He then worked in his father's leather shop for $800 a year. When the Civil War began in 1861, the army was not interested in him, but in June 1861, he was appointed a colonel in the 21st Illinois Volunteers. In August, he was made a brigadier general of troops in Illinois and Missouri; then his career took off. He won well-publicized victories at Forts Henry and Donelson in Tennessee. Promoted to major general, he won at the battle of Shiloh in Tennessee and then laid siege to the Confederate stronghold at Vicksburg, Mississippi. Victory at Chattanooga drove the rebel troops out of Tennessee, and Lincoln named Grant lieutenant general in charge of all Union troops.

A long series of bloody battles followed as Grant tangled with the Confederate General Robert E. Lee. Finally, Lee's troops headed westward, but they were cut off. Grant met with Lee and offered generous surrender terms. The war continued, but for all intents, the South had lost.

President Johnson and General Grant came to distrust each other, and by 1868, it was clear that Grant would receive the Republican nomination for president. Running with him was Schuyler Colfax, Speaker of the House. The Democratic candidate, Horatio Seymour, had little chance of winning, and carried only eight states. The popular vote was much closer; Grant won with only a 300,000 vote margin.

GRANT AS PRESIDENT. Unlike Johnson, Grant was willing to let Congress lead in making laws. He often chose friends for high positions; unfortunately, many of them abused his friendship by participating in crooked schemes. Since he had always been poor, Grant was impressed by the way rich people lived, and he assumed that they were smarter than he. Grant listened to their explanations of why certain policies should be developed, not realizing he was being taken in.

An example occurred when Jim Fisk and Jay Gould persuaded Grant that the government should not sell its gold reserves. Their goal was to drive the price of gold up, and they knew that if the government started selling gold, the price would drop. The president's brother-in-law was also involved. When newspapers found out what was happening, Grant had to release the gold and prices dropped.

Other scandals embarrassed Grant. The Credit Mobilier scandal involved bribes to government officials from the Union Pacific Railroad not to investigate fraud in the construction of the Union Pacific. Another scandal involved the Whiskey Ring, a group of whiskey distillers, revenue collectors, and high federal officials, who conspired to avoid taxation through fraudulent reports on whiskey production. They had bribed the president's personal secretary and had given Grant a beautiful team of horses. The secretary of war was found to have received bribes for giving Indian trading post rights to crooks.

Members of Congress were little better than the administration, and often they were paid by special interests to offer bills they wanted. City and state governments were also low on morality; the most famous example was the Tweed Ring that ran New York City's Democratic Party. Boss Tweed was finally sent to jail.

Many people ignored the corruption and were more concerned about other events of the time. The transcontinental railroad to California was finished in 1869. In 1873, a major financial panic occurred that closed many shops and stores and caused mass unemployment.

Southern Reconstruction was meeting armed resistance from the secret terror organization, the Ku Klux Klan (KKK). The Klan wore hoods and sheets over their bodies and terrorized blacks who tried to vote. Riots became common in the South, and Union troops could not control them. Since many of these governments were corrupt, the public eventually concluded it was time to restore state government to Southerners. In 1876, both parties' candidates proposed an end to Reconstruction.

In 1876, the Republicans refused to give Grant a third nomination, and he left office in 1877. After leaving office, the Grants went on a long trip around the world and were greeted as heroes. Grant's financial situation worsened, and in 1884, he lost most of his money. Desperate to provide an income for his wife, he wrote his autobiography. It was not published until after he died. It became a best seller, and his family earned $450,000 from it in the first two years.

RUTHERFORD B. HAYES
(1822–1893, P. 1877–1881)

The election of 1876 took place in the year of the nation's centennial. Instead of showing how well democracy worked, it was an embarrassing display of dirty politics, ending with a controversial outcome. Both candidates were noted for their honesty, but their parties engaged in dirty politics. In the end, Rutherford B. Hayes was chosen, not by the people, but by Congress.

Hayes was born in Ohio in 1822; shortly after his birth, his father died, and he was raised by an overly-protective mother and older sister. He graduated from Kenyon College in 1842 and then attended Harvard Law School. After five years in a small town law practice, he moved to Cincinnati, where his law career was very successful. He met and eventually married Lucy Webb; their marriage produced a daughter and seven sons.

Hayes was a Whig until the Republican party formed. His only political office before the Civil War was as city solicitor. When war came, he enlisted as a major and ended the war as a major general of volunteers. He was in the thick of battles and was wounded five times. In 1864, while he was still in the army, he was elected to the U.S. House. He then resigned from the army. While he supported his party, he did not like the angry atmosphere of the contest between Congress and President Johnson. In 1867, he left Congress to serve as governor of Ohio. Even though he took the unpopular position that blacks should be allowed to vote, he had won the governorship by 3,000 votes.

During his first two terms as governor (1867–1871), Hayes pushed for reforms. He wanted civil service reform and voter registration to prevent vote fraud; he improved conditions in prisons and insane asylums; he established railroad regulation and granted approval of the Fifteenth Amendment. In 1872, he ran for the U.S. House, but he lost because voters were still angry over the corruption in the Grant administration, so they did not vote for Republican candidates. In 1875, Hayes won a third term as governor, and he was immediately picked as a possible contender for the Republican nomination for president.

The Republican Convention had two popular men to choose between: James G. Blaine and Hayes. There were accusations that Speaker Blaine had received bribes from railroads. He denied it, but many did not believe him. Hayes had been honest throughout his career and was the safer choice to face the Democrats.

The Democratic choice was Samuel Tilden, governor of New York, who had thrown Boss Tweed into prison and cleaned up corruption. Both Hayes and Tilden wanted to end Reconstruction, and they favored civil service reform. If left to the candidates, the campaign would have been clean. Their enthusiastic supporters, however, were determined that their respective parties must win and so engaged in dirty politics.

Democrats pointed out the corruption of the Grant administration, and of Republican "carpetbag" governments in the South, supported by federal troops. Republican speakers often brought up the Civil War issue to remind voters that Copperhead Democrats had opposed the war and that Lincoln was a Republican killed by a Democrat.

As telegraph messages brought in election results from across the country, it appeared Tilden had won. It was clear that Tilden had 184 electoral votes and Hayes had 165. However, there was still some room to question the results in states with 20 more electoral votes. Many strange incidents had occurred in some Southern states: ballots had disappeared, ballot boxes had been stuffed, and voters had been threatened. The Republican chairman announced Hayes had won. Both parties sent "statesmen" to the Southern states, but their findings were all by party lines. Democrats were sure they had won, and Republicans said that many Republican voters had been scared off by violent Democrats.

To solve the problem, Congress created the Electoral Commission. It consisted of seven Democrats, seven Republicans, and an independent, Justice David Davis of the Supreme Court. When Illinois named Davis as governor, he quickly accepted. All the other justices on the Court were Republicans, but Justice Joseph Bradley was appointed to the Commission, giving the Republicans a majority on the Commission. After investigating the returns in the three disputed states (South Carolina, Louisiana, and Florida), the Commission concluded by an eight to seven vote in each case that Hayes had won. The totals were 185 for Hayes to 184 for Tilden. Congress finally declared Hayes the winner on March 2, 1877, two days before the president was to be inaugurated.

HAYES AS PRESIDENT. Democrats were unhappy, and they referred to Hayes as "Old 8 to 7." However, Hayes appointed able and honest men to his cabinet, and he withdrew federal troops from the South as he had promised. White Democrats took charge in all Southern states. In 1877, Hayes issued an executive order forbidding federal employees from taking part in political organizations.

Since Hayes and his wife were active in the temperance movement, no alcohol was served at White House gatherings. When lemonade replaced liquor, Hayes' wife was referred to as "Lemonade Lucy." One of her contributions was the hosting of the Easter egg roll on the White House lawn.

Hayes was not an outgoing man who could gain wide public support, although he did have the support of Mark Twain. Party leaders who depended on the spoils system to get support were very unhappy with Hayes; so were those Californians who wanted the government to stop Chinese from immigrating to the United States. After workers rioted in several cities, Hayes sent troops to restore order.

After his term, Hayes said: "No one ever left the presidency with less disappointment, fewer heartburnings or more general content than I do." His wife died in 1889, and he died in 1893. His main contributions to the presidency were to restore respect for government and to end Reconstruction.

8 TO 7 ELECTORAL COMMISSION VICTORY FOR HAYES!

Name: _____ Date: _____

Points to Ponder (Reconstruction Presidents: A. Johnson, Grant, Hayes)

1. What made Johnson different from other Southerners in Congress in 1861?

   _____

   _____

   _____

2. What law got Johnson into trouble? How close did he come to losing his office as president?

   _____

   _____

   _____

3. Why was Grant's name changed to U.S. Grant?

   _____

   _____

   _____

4. How was Grant's career going before the war came?

   _____

   _____

   _____

5. Why was Grant less successful as president than he had been as a general?

   _____

   _____

   _____

   _____

Name: _____ Date: _____

Points to Ponder (Reconstruction Presidents: A. Johnson, Grant, Hayes)

6. How did the Ku Klux Klan interfere with Reconstruction?

   _____

   _____

   _____

   _____

   _____

7. What part had Hayes played in the Civil War?

   _____

   _____

   _____

8. Why was Hayes chosen as the Republican candidate over the better-known Blaine?

   _____

   _____

   _____

   _____

☆ ☆ ☆   **Explore History**   ☆ ☆ ☆

1. Have a class debate about Black Codes. Were they fair or necessary? Compare slaves' lives before and after they were freed. What were some of the laws for freed slaves?

2. Discuss the carpetbaggers, their effect on Reconstruction, and their work with emancipated slaves.

3. What was the purpose of the Freedmen's Bureau? Make a poster about the ways it helped slaves after the war.

4. Compare and discuss the Hayes/Tilden election with the election of 2000 between Al Gore and George W. Bush.

5. Write a mini-report on the history of Alaska. Include who sold it to the United States and how much was paid for it.

JAMES GARFIELD
(1831–1881, P. 1881)

Many officeholders claim that they did not "seek the office, the office sought them." For that to happen in the case of a city councilman or mayor is not unusual, but no one since Washington had ever been chosen for president by his political party without wanting the nomination. Garfield was an exception.

Garfield was born in 1831 in a log cabin on the Ohio frontier. His father died when he was two years old, and the family struggled to survive. To support his mother, James worked for farmers in the area; he also attended public school. When he was 16, he left home, dreaming of going to sea. He worked on a lake schooner for a short time but lost that job. Then he worked on the canal as a driver and helmsman. After a short time in college, he began teaching in a rural school, then he returned to Western Reserve Eclectic Institute (now Hiram College) in Ohio.

In 1854, Garfield transferred to Williams College, graduated, and returned as president of the Eclectic Institute. With a faculty of five members, he spent more time teaching than sitting in an office. He loved languages and taught Latin, Greek, and German, as well as history and English. In addition to teaching, he became a popular Disciples of Christ preacher and delivered excellent sermons. In 1859, he married Lucretia Rudolph, and he left the classroom to become a state senator. While there, he studied law and passed the bar exam in 1860.

When the Civil War came, Garfield volunteered and took command as colonel of the 42nd Ohio Volunteers. He knew nothing about military organization and strategy when he became an officer, but he worked hard and learned quickly. His first battle was in Kentucky against a West Pointer, and Garfield won. His victory was noticed, and he was promoted to brigadier general. In 1862, Garfield was elected to the U.S. House even though he told the voters he would return to the army. In 1863, he served as General W.S. Rosecrans's chief of staff during the battle at Chickamauga. He entered the House in 1863 and was appointed to the Committee on Military Affairs. In September of that year, he became a major general but resigned from the army in December to take his seat in the House.

Garfield became one of the leaders of the House because of his speaking ability and his study of the issues. Together with Speaker James G. Blaine, he led the party during the Grant administration. Garfield served on major committees and became well acquainted with the workings of the government. His reputation for honesty and hard work made him well known. By 1880, he was House minority leader.

The Republican Party was badly divided going into the election of 1880. A group called "Stalwarts" favored nominating former President Grant, but the "Half-breeds" favored Blaine. Garfield was a Half-breed, and they succeeded in stopping Grant at the 1880 convention. Blaine supporters could not win the nomination either, and on the 34th ballot, a few votes were cast for Garfield. He protested that his name had been mentioned without his consent. Garfield was chosen on the 36th ballot. He was stunned at first, and then said: "Get me out of here!" For vice president, the convention chose Chester Arthur.

The Democratic candidate, Winfield Hancock, had been a military hero, and had won great praise for setting up the defenses at Gettysburg. He had little political record and few enemies in the party.

Both parties were guilty of dirty politics. Some Republicans called Hancock a coward who had no knowledge of the major issues. The Democrats charged that Garfield had received a $329 dividend from the corrupt Credit Mobilier, but they could not prove it. They began putting "329" on buildings and storefronts. Chester Arthur, who had been fired by President Hayes from his job as customs collector, was an easy target for scandalmongers. The Democrats even manufactured an issue. A letter was forged in Garfield's handwriting stating he favored bringing cheap Chinese laborers to California. The letter had two misspellings in it; Garfield's ability to spell was well known, and it may have worked against Hancock.

Garfield used his knowledge of German in the campaign, and he sometimes spoke in German to immigrant audiences. The election was very close, and he beat Hancock by only 10,000 popular votes. His electoral vote majority was much higher, and he won by 214–155.

GARFIELD AS PRESIDENT. Garfield's main problem as president was the split in his party and the choice of men for high positions. The leader of the Stalwarts, Senator Roscoe Conkling of New York, was furious when Garfield chose Blaine to be secretary of state. He became livid when Garfield replaced a Conkling supporter as customs collector for the Port of New York with a Blaine man. There were 1,300 jobs affected by that decision. Conkling and the other New York senator, Tom Platt, resigned. To their surprise, they were not re-elected by the legislature.

Garfield had made an important point. The president usually asked senators of his party who they thought should fill government posts. By this victory, Garfield established the principle that appointments are the choice of the president, not the senators.

As Garfield walked through the Washington railroad station in July 1881, he was shot by a disappointed office seeker, Charles Guiteau, who had been turned down for the post of consul at Paris. As Guiteau was being wrestled down, he shouted out: "I am a Stalwart, and now Arthur is president." Guiteau was later found guilty of murder and hanged in 1882.

The president was not dead, however, and he was moved to the seashore of New Jersey to escape the heat of the summer in Washington. Garfield died in September 1881.

CHESTER ARTHUR
(1830–1886, P. 1881–1885)

In 1881, President Garfield was shot by an assassin who said: "I am a Stalwart, and now Arthur is president." For weeks, Garfield's health declined. During that time, there were no cabinet meetings or other official functions, and then the sad news came that Garfield had died. Now, the choice of an assassin was president. Few expected much of Arthur. His whole public life had been tied to the Conkling political machine in New York, and everyone viewed him as a puppet of Roscoe Conkling. It was a poor way to become president.

Arthur was born in Fairfield, Vermont, near the Canadian border. His father was an Irish-born Baptist preacher, and he moved his family five times in the first nine years of Chester's life. The Arthurs settled down at Union Village, New York, for five years and then moved to Schenectady. Chester taught school while helping pay his way through Union College, from which he graduated in 1848. He continued teaching while he studied law and became a lawyer in 1854. He was a successful lawyer and prospered. He married Ellen Herndon, the daughter of a naval officer, in 1859.

In 1860, the governor of New York appointed Arthur engineer-in-chief of the state militia as a political favor. When the Civil War began, he was put in charge of feeding, housing, and supplying army recruits who were passing through New York City. It was a major responsibility, and he carried it out well. During the war, he made friends with many important people and began to move up in Republican politics.

Getting rich was very much in style. Some made fortunes in business. Large corporations often used tactics that were dishonest to break competitors. There were fortunes in gold and silver mining or large western cattle ranches. Land speculation near cities made fortunes for many. Cities were growing rapidly, and improvements in streets, water systems, and transportation were needed. The poor needed relief and jobs. All of those needing a friendly law or a government contract turned to politicians for help.

Receiving gifts and bribes became a welcome source of income for state, local, and even federal employees. Those who had been helped were expected to get out to vote and contribute to campaign funds for the party and officials who helped them. If the party or candidate lost the election, they were no longer able to give favors, and the money and support shifted to the other party.

Corrupt party machines were present in both the major parties. The Tammany Hall Democratic politicians competed against the Roscoe Conkling Republican machine. When Conkling delivered the New York vote to President Grant, Conkling had great influence in the federal government. He picked Arthur to be collector of customs for the Port of New York. The job paid well and gave 1,300 jobs to loyal party workers. Arthur, then chairman of the Republican state committee, had received his reward for service to Conkling and the party.

When Democrats won New York state elections in 1874, anti-Conkling Republican leaders decided it was time to weaken his influence in the party, and they started with the customs house. Hayes ordered that no federal employee could engage in politics. Arthur refused to resign, claiming that he had done nothing worse than had been done before, and he was not responsible for the system. The president fired him in July 1878.

Conkling was not finished in politics; in 1879, one of his supporters was elected governor, and in 1880, Conkling was chosen for the Senate. He led the Stalwarts (Grant supporters) at the Republican Convention of 1880. Their goal was to nominate Grant for a third term.

After James Garfield, a Half-Breed (an anti-Grant reformer) won the nomination, the Reform Republicans realized Stalwart support was needed to win the election. A Stalwart leader suggested Arthur for vice president. Conkling told Arthur to refuse the offer, but Arthur accepted it anyway. It was a higher job than he had ever expected to hold. Reform Republicans did not like Arthur, but they could not afford for the party to dump him. After Garfield won, most people still considered Arthur a Conkling puppet.

Garfield appointed Reform Republicans to federal jobs in New York over the protests of Conkling. Then came Charles Guiteau's shooting of the president, and his statement: "I am a Stalwart, and now Arthur is president." As Garfield slowly died, the nation realized that Arthur was going to be the next president.

ARTHUR AS PRESIDENT. Arthur overcame the fears that he would be guided by Conkling. Ohio's governor said people were going to see a difference between Vice President Arthur and President Arthur. He was right. Arthur was careful to choose able Republicans for office, but he ignored most requests from Conkling.

The assassination of Garfield caused a public demand for an end to the spoils system. In 1883, Democrats gained control of Congress and passed the Pendleton Civil Service Act. It created a Civil Service Commission; examinations were now required for about ten percent of government jobs. It was the beginning of the end of the spoils system. Arthur strongly supported the Pendleton Act.

Mail service was improved, and postage stamps were dropped from three cents to two cents. Congress appropriated money for new steel ships to replace the old wooden ships of the Civil War era. Major improvements were made at the White House, and boxes of junk left behind from previous residents of the mansion were carted off. Dinners and social events returned. Arthur's wife had died before he became president, but he and his sister were fine hosts.

Arthur was not nominated for re-election in 1884, and he died in 1886.

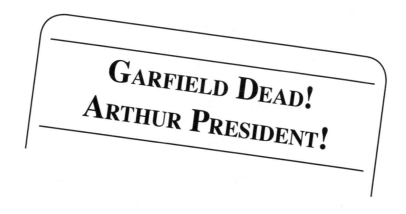

GARFIELD DEAD!
ARTHUR PRESIDENT!

GROVER CLEVELAND
(1837–1908, P. 1885–1889, 1893–1897)

In 1885, when Cleveland took the oath of office as president, he was the first Democrat since the Civil War to be elected, the first man who had no military record to be chosen since Buchanan, and the only president to rise from being mayor, to governor, to president in just two years.

Grover was born in New Jersey, the son of a Presbyterian minister. His father died when he was 16, and Grover worked for a while at a school for the blind. He borrowed $25 and headed west with a friend. He got as far as Buffalo, New York, where an uncle helped him get a job in a law firm. There were several unusual qualities about Cleveland. He was very determined and often worked all night without sleep. He did not like anything that wasted time, which included the limits he placed on his social life. A wife and family would take time, so he postponed marriage until much later.

Cleveland was very independent. When he began practicing law in 1859, clients found he was an excellent lawyer. He kept his fees low, but expected no interference from his clients.

When the Civil War came, he hired a substitute to fight for him. This was perfectly legal, and he explained he did it because he supported his widowed mother. He was a loyal Democrat, and in 1862 he was named as a ward supervisor, then an assistant district attorney. He then ran for district attorney in 1865; from that time until 1870, he worked at building up his law practice.

Cleveland was elected sheriff of Buffalo County in 1871. He did not believe in making others do the difficult jobs, so he performed two hangings himself. After three years as sheriff, he returned to private law practice.

In 1881, Buffalo reformers wanted to find a candidate for mayor who not only had political experience but was honest. Cleveland became their candidate, and he won. As mayor, he rejected costly street cleaning and sewer contracts.

In 1882, Cleveland was elected governor of New York with the motto: "A public office is a public trust." Again, he became famous for what he did not do. He did not allow the passing of costly spending bills that would help special interests. He refused to work with the Tammany Hall Democratic machine. He was now beginning to draw national support from reformers.

The Republican Convention met first in 1884, and the party quickly chose James G. Blaine, the most famous party leader of the time. However, Blaine's reputation had been tarnished by charges that he had received bribes from railroads. The Democrats chose Grover Cleveland, a man noted for his honesty. As soon as Cleveland was chosen, Reform Republicans, called "mugwumps," switched parties to support him.

The 1884 campaign. The campaign became the dirtiest to date. Democrats chanted: "Blaine, Blaine, James G. Blaine! The continental liar from the state of Maine." Then Republicans discovered that Cleveland had paid child support to an alcoholic widow and her son. When Cleveland was asked what to do about the charge, he said: "Tell the truth." Opponents made up jokes about him, but others supported him because he did not lie.

Blaine made two mistakes that hurt him badly. He was at a Republican rally where a Presbyterian minister said that a vote for Cleveland was a vote for "rum, Romanism (Catholic Church), and rebellion." Blaine said nothing against it at the time, but it turned many Catholics against him. That same evening, Blaine attended a dinner hosted by wealthy supporters. There was a depression at the time, and Blaine's remarks about "Republican prosperity" that night did not help him.

The election was very close, but Cleveland won 217–184 in electoral votes; in New York state, he won by only 1,100 votes.

CLEVELAND AS PRESIDENT (first term). Cleveland's motto could have been: "When in doubt, say NO!" An example of this was his attitude toward veteran pensions. He had not served in the war, and Republican politicians were quick to point that out. Still, he had the courage to turn down individual pensions that had no merit. One family asked for a pension for a man who drowned while deserting. A widow claimed a pension for her husband who died in 1883 from a hernia he had in 1863. He also vetoed pensions for all veterans with disabilities, whether they had been disabled during the war or after. The pension issue probably hurt him in 1888.

Because the government was taking in more money than it spent, Cleveland recommended cutting the taxes on imports. When advisors warned them this would hurt in Northern industrial states, he answered: "What is the use of being elected and re-elected unless you stand for something?"

Public lands were being used by lumber companies and cattle ranchers. The government ordered cattle off government land and stopped lumbering operations. This policy change hurt Cleveland in the West.

Cleveland never showed much imagination in creating new programs. Some changes occurred with little or no help from him. The building of a new navy had started with Arthur; it was continued by Cleveland's secretary of the navy. The Interstate Commerce Act was passed in 1887 and gave the government the power to regulate interstate railroads.

In Cleveland's personal life, the biggest change was getting married. The bride was 21-year-old Frances Folsom, his law partner's daughter. Her father had named her Cleveland's ward upon his death. They were married in the White House while John Philip Sousa's band played the wedding march. Cleveland was easier to get along with after the marriage, and he even took more vacations. He still worked long hours, going to bed between 2:00 and 3:00 A.M.

After losing the election of 1888, Cleveland told the White House staff to take care of the furnishings. He wanted everything the same when he returned four years later.

Cleveland's second term follows Harrison's presidency.

Name: _____ Date: _____

Points to Ponder (Garfield, Arthur, Cleveland)

1. Garfield was the fourth president to die in office. Who were the others who had died before him?

   _____

   _____

2. What do you think of the moral standards of government in that time?

   _____

   _____

   _____

3. Do you think Arthur was more like Garfield or Conkling when he became president? Why?

   _____

   _____

   _____

4. How did Cleveland lose popularity in the West?

   _____

   _____

5. What was the importance of the Interstate Commerce Act?

   _____

   _____

   _____

 **Explore History**

1. Compare the "Stalwarts" and "Half-Breeds." How did the split between Stalwarts and Half-Breeds affect Garfield's administration? How did the struggle between them affect the choice of Arthur for vice president? Discuss the corrupt political machines of Roscoe Conkling and Boss Tweed.

2. Write a short biography on John Philip Sousa. What songs and marches made him famous? Try to find recordings of some of his marches and play them for the class.

3. Pretend you are interviewing President Arthur regarding the Pendleton Civil Service Act. How did it affect the spoils system?

BENJAMIN HARRISON
(1833–1901, P. 1889–1893)

On election night in 1889, the nation waited in suspense for the returns in what was obviously going to be a close race for president. Benjamin Harrison waited for the Indiana returns, heard that he had won the state, and said he was going to bed. He was asked why. He said that if he lost, there was nothing he could do about it, and if he won, tomorrow would be a busy day. He won, and the next four years were busy.

Benjamin was the grandson of William Henry Harrison, and he was born on his grandfather's estate in 1833. His father had been affected by hard times but provided him with a tutor as well as public school education. Benjamin attended Farmer's College for a time and then graduated from Miami University (Ohio) in 1852. He then studied law and became a lawyer in 1854. He joined the Republican Party because of the slavery issue and soon became one of its most effective public speakers.

In 1862, Harrison was appointed colonel of the 70th Indiana Infantry. He knew nothing about war, and his troops knew even less. He was hard on his men and was not popular, but he did mold them into disciplined soldiers. In 1864, they were with Sherman in the battles around Atlanta. He left the army in 1865 as a brevet (temporary) brigadier general.

Harrison returned to his law practice and family. He and his wife, Caroline, whom he had married in 1853, had two children. Harrison was active in Republican politics, and as chairman of the state delegation to the convention in 1880, helped Garfield win the nomination. Harrison entered the U.S. Senate in 1880. When the Democrats won control of Indiana's legislature, Harrison lost his seat in 1886. After James G. Blaine decided not to run again, he suggested that Harrison be the party nominee for president in 1888. He was chosen on the eighth ballot. The Democrats ran Cleveland again.

Much of the support for Harrison's campaign came from wealthy backers. The $3 million raised was the largest fund ever raised to that time. Harrison did his campaigning from his front porch. Groups would come, he would say a few words, and they would leave. Not only did Cleveland not campaign, but he would not let cabinet members campaign for him. Harrison won the electoral vote 233–168, but Cleveland won the popular vote by 100,000.

HARRISON AS PRESIDENT. Harrison chose competent people for his administration, but the only one who was well known was James G. Blaine, the new secretary of state. However, Harrison was never able to take charge. In his first two years, Speaker of the House Thomas ("Czar") Reed was more the leader than he was. He established the "Reed Rules" that made every member vote, and that anyone present was counted, whether they answered the roll call or not. He developed the committee system that is still used. The main interests of Republicans were veterans' pensions and high tariffs.

Under the new pension plan, any man who had served 90 days and was now physically or mentally disabled was eligible for a pension. It did not matter whether the disability was related to his military service. The widows and children of veterans also received pensions.

To get the high tariff they wanted, the Republican leaders had to pass laws other members wanted. Some wanted to control big business. In 1890, Congress passed the Sherman Antitrust Act. It defined as a trust "any contract or combination in restraint of trade." Reformers thought this was an important first step, but the law was almost impossible to enforce.

To satisfy silver producers and farmers who wanted more money in circulation, the Sherman Silver Purchase Act was passed. It guaranteed the government would buy more silver to be made into coins.

The McKinley tariff was the highest tax on imports yet. Passed in 1890, its taxes were set by American industries to keep foreign competition out. It worked like this: an English company produces widgets for 50 cents at a profit; an American company produces them at a bigger profit for $1.00. To keep English widgets out, a tax of 70 cents is put on them. The American widget buyer pays $1.00 for a widget he could have bought for half that price without the tariff. Businesses and workers in industrial states favored it, while consumers in farm states opposed it.

The White House was renovated during Harrison's term. The kitchen and heating system were improved, rooms were painted, and private bathrooms were installed in each bedroom. Electric lights were installed, but after a few shocks, Harrison told his family to let the staff turn them on and off. If they forgot, the lights stayed on all night.

With more money coming in, Congress started spending more on "pork barrel projects" (those projects helping their state or district) like river and road improvements. Government was spending $989 million, and people started calling it the "billion-dollar Congress." Reed said this was a billion-dollar country and needed the money. The public disagreed.

The Democrats took control of the House in 1890, and for his last two years as president, Harrison achieved very little. Harrison did little to make friends with either party in Congress. He refused to waste time chatting. He kept only one chair in his office so guests did not stay too long. When senators spoke to him, he did not answer.

Cleveland returns. After losing the 1888 election, Cleveland had returned to his law practice. Anger over the McKinley tariff persuaded him to try for a second term as president in 1892, and the Democrats quickly chose him; his running mate was Adlai Stevenson of Illinois. Harrison was chosen again as the Republican nominee, but since his wife was very ill, he did not even give front porch speeches.

A new party, the Populists, met in Omaha, Nebraska, for their first national convention. They were mostly farmers who were angry with both parties. They wanted changes: senators to be elected by the people, a graduated income tax, government-owned railroads, and most of all, the unlimited coinage of silver. With more money in circulation, it would be easier for them to pay off their debts. Their candidate was James Weaver.

Cleveland won easily over Harrison; 277–145 in electoral votes, and 380,000 popular votes. Harrison went back to private law practice, made a fortune, and wrote books. His first wife had died in 1892. He remarried in 1896. He began to relax and became more considerate and kind.

GROVER CLEVELAND
(second term 1893–1897)

Many Cleveland supporters wanted the tariff lowered, but other issues became more important: economic collapse, labor strikes, and foreign issues. Cleveland took charge of everything, answered the White House phone himself, and did not use secretaries. However, as new problems arose, Cleveland unfortunately used old methods to meet them, which did not work.

Much of the economic growth of the 1870–1890 period had been in railroad construction. Over 70,000 miles of track had been laid between 1880 and 1890. Now, railroads had either completed construction or could not borrow enough money to finish laying track. Because of this, unemployment spread, which in turn affected industries like steel and coal that depended on railroads for much of their business. Those who had money stopped spending, fearing hard times ahead. About 2.5 million workers lost their jobs. Jacob Coxey, a reformer, proposed that the unemployed be hired to build roads. He led an "army" of about 400 tired and hungry men to hold a demonstration in Washington. Coxey was arrested for walking on the White House lawn.

Workers at Pullman's Railroad Car factory had their wages cut, and they went on strike. They were supported by the American Railway Union. ARU members working for railroads refused to attach Pullman cars to trains. Attorney General Richard Olney persuaded Cleveland to crack down on the workers. Accused of interfering with the transport of mail, the union was ordered back to work. When the strike continued, the union president, Eugene Debs, was sent to prison for six months.

Instead of spending money to help the unemployed or listening to worker complaints, Cleveland said the financial crisis was caused by too much money in circulation. The government stopped buying silver to make money. With tax revenue dropping, Cleveland built up the gold supply by selling bonds, and turned to the big banker, J. P. Morgan, for help.

Many Americans were outraged. One of these, William Jennings Bryan, attacked Cleveland policies at the Democratic Convention in 1896, and he became the party candidate for president. The Republicans chose William McKinley as their nominee.

After his term ended, Cleveland moved to Princeton, New Jersey. There was some talk of him running again in 1904; while he was flattered, Cleveland made no effort to win the nomination. He died in 1908.

In his two terms as president, Cleveland had been stubbornly honest, but he had provided little leadership in solving the economic crisis that brought disaster to millions.

Name: _____ Date: _____

Points to Ponder (B. Harrison, Cleveland)

1. If you had supported Harrison in 1892, what are two things you might have used to convince others to vote for him?

_____

_____

_____

2. Why did wealthy industrial leaders like high tariffs? _____

_____

_____

3. Why would consumers like low tariffs? _____

_____

_____

4. Why did a slowdown in railroad construction hurt the economy?

_____

_____

5. What did Coxey want to do? What happened to him? _____

_____

_____

6. Do you think Harrison or Cleveland could be elected today? Why or why not?

_____

_____

_____

☆ ☆ ☆ **Explore History** ☆ ☆ ☆

1. Draw a picture or make a diorama of a Pullman train car, or pretend you are interviewing President Cleveland or Eugene Debs and write a newspaper article about the American Railway Union strike.

2. Write a short biography on Thomas "Czar" Reed.

3. John Sherman was the younger brother of General William T. Sherman. Make a time line of his career or write a report on the Sherman Antitrust Act and the Silver Purchase Act.

WILLIAM McKINLEY
(1843–1901, P. 1897–1901)

By the late 1890s, there were two Americas in one nation. First, there were the "captains of industry" who had riches, power, and influence. Government had been very friendly to them in recent years. They believed government should let business grow without interference.

Secondly, there were others who worked 70 to 80 hours a week and lived in poverty in cities. There were also farmers working from sunrise to sunset, with little profit for their efforts. Radicals, called anarchists, wanted to destroy government; socialists wanted government to take over the railroads, telephone, and telegraph companies and to place heavy taxes on the wealthy. More common were those who wanted business restricted by tightly-enforced new laws. The Sherman Antitrust law was a joke, and they knew it. New, tougher laws, however, could give the average person a more even playing field. The election of 1896 gave the voters a clear choice of which way the nation should go.

William McKinley was born in Ohio in 1843. He was intelligent as a child, and his mother hoped he would become a Methodist minister. He only had one year of college before he became ill and had to leave. After recovering, he taught school and was a post office clerk. When the Civil War came, he enlisted in the 23rd Ohio Volunteer Infantry Regiment, serving under Rutherford B. Hayes. McKinley left the army as a major.

After the war, McKinley became a lawyer and was active in Republican politics. He married Ida Saxton in 1871, and the couple had two daughters, both of whom died before they were four years old. Mrs. McKinley became epileptic and mentally depressed. William took care of her the rest of her life without ever complaining.

McKinley was elected to the U.S. House in 1876. He served there until he lost the election in 1882 and then again from 1886 to 1890. In 1890, he wrote the McKinley tariff, which made him the friend of many wealthy industrialists. One of them, Mark Hanna, began pushing for him to be the party candidate for president someday. McKinley served as two-term governor of Ohio from 1891 to 1895. When Ohio coal miners went out on strike, he called out the National Guard to put down violence, but he also raised money to buy food for starving strikers.

In 1896, McKinley was chosen by the Republicans, whose platform opposed silver money and favored gold. They knew this would cost them the West but hoped to convince Eastern workers gold money was good for them. The Democrats were split on the issue between "goldbugs" of the East and silver supporters from the West. At the Democratic Convention, William J. Bryan gave his famous "Cross of Gold" speech. It was so outstanding that he was chosen as the party's 1896 candidate.

The 1896 campaign. It was a dramatic campaign. Bryan traveled around the country speaking to crowds gathered at railroad stations. He argued that with more money in circulation, there is a better chance for everyone to get money. McKinley spent his time giving little speeches to crowds who came by train to hear him. Hanna was out raising money to hire speakers and pay for rallies and campaign advertising. McKinley won by 600,000 popular votes, and 271–196 in electoral votes.

McKINLEY AS PRESIDENT. McKinley had a friendly Republican Congress to work with, and he was much smoother with them than Harrison had been. Even when someone came into his office angry, McKinley greeted them with a smile; when they left, they were smiling too, wearing one of his red carnations in their lapel. He was not good at delegating authority, and he did not let his cabinet make decisions that were unpopular with the public.

Instead of the usual tax or gold-silver issues, attention turned to the rising troubles in Spanish-owned Cuba. Cubans revolted against Spain in 1895, and American newspapers told how cruelly the Cuban people were treated. They found that newspaper sales soared with these stories, some of which were true and others of which were greatly exaggerated. The battleship *Maine* was sent to Havana to protect American lives and property. An insulting letter written by a Spanish official, calling McKinley "weak and a bidder for the admiration of the crowd" was published in American newspapers. Americans began calling for war with Spain.

On February 15, 1898, the *Maine* exploded, and over 250 officers and men were killed. Most Americans were convinced the Spanish had done it, and the call for war was greater than before. McKinley did not favor war but found he was almost alone in opposing it. Southerners, northerners, and westerners joined in the demand for war. In April, McKinley asked Congress to declare war. Ten days later, Congress approved.

The Spanish-American War. The navy was in better shape to begin the war than the army. Admiral George Dewey attacked Manila Bay as soon as he could and won an easy victory. A fleet under William Sampson blockaded a Spanish fleet at Santiago Bay in Cuba; when the Spanish tried to escape, they were badly beaten.

The U.S. Army was small and was built up by state national guards and volunteer units. The most famous of these was Theodore Roosevelt's Rough Riders. Their charge up San Juan Hill thrilled the nation. Spain surrendered in August. The peace treaty gave Cuba, Puerto Rico, Guam, and the Philippines to the United States. Spain received $20 million. The United States gave Cuba independence in 1901.

McKinley easily won re-election in 1900. In 1901 while he was in Buffalo, New York, he was shot and killed by an anarchist, Leon Czolgosz. His vice president, Theodore Roosevelt, was sworn in as the next president, and the United States entered the twentieth century with a dynamic new leader.

THEODORE ROOSEVELT
(1858–1919, P. 1901–1909)

There was never a president quite like Theodore Roosevelt. To most Americans, he was a human tornado, always picking things up and never dropping them in the same place. They liked his energy, his devotion to public service, and his desire to bring the United States to its just place as a leader among the nations. To his enemies, he was a source of irritation who did not know when to stop. The press loved him, and he used the press to get his message across. For the first time, reporters were assigned to the White House to gather news.

Roosevelt's life was a constant struggle to prove himself. His parents were wealthy and prominent. He was descended from Dutch aristocrats on his father's side and distinguished Georgians on his mother's side. Theodore suffered from poor eyesight and asthma; to help him breathe on muggy summer nights, his father took him on long carriage rides. After he was beaten up by some bullies, Theodore took up boxing and proudly showed his black eye to an aunt. He loved to read history and natural science; he was especially fond of birds.

Roosevelt graduated from Harvard in 1880 and married Alice Lee. He tried studying law, but did not like it, so he became a writer. His first book was published in 1882, *The Naval War of 1812.* He loved history but did not want to teach it. He was elected to the New York legislature where he served from 1882 to 1884. He often held press interviews where he talked about misconduct of legislators, the needs of workers, and better government for New York City. In 1883, he bought a ranch in the Dakota Territory. It was not financially profitable, but his asthma improved, he mixed with cowboys, and proved himself capable of hardy living. He once chased outlaws through a blizzard.

In 1884, Roosevelt's wife died in childbirth on the same day his mother died. He retreated for a time to Dakota Territory, pulled himself together, and campaigned for James G. Blaine in the fall. He did not like Blaine, but he disliked the "mugwumps," who had deserted the party more. After the election, he returned to writing, and between 1885 and 1889, he wrote seven books. In 1886, he came in third in the mayor's race in New York City. He then went to London where he married Edith Carow. In 1888, he supported Harrison, and was given a job as civil service commissioner in 1889. While in that position, he fought political influence in granting jobs and made civil service tests more practical.

The reform mayor of New York City made Roosevelt police commissioner in 1895. Roosevelt put in a merit system for promotions, fought graft, and fired policemen who were not doing their job. Since many policemen had been given their jobs by political leaders, the leaders were not happy with Roosevelt's interference. They suggested to President McKinley that he find a good job for Roosevelt in Washington.

In 1897, McKinley appointed him assistant secretary of the navy. Roosevelt was one of those most anxious to declare war on Spain. One day, while his boss was out, he sent a message to Admiral Dewey that in case of war with Spain he was to sail immediately and attack Manila Bay. When war came, Roosevelt resigned to organize the Rough Riders. At first, he was second in command under Colonel Leonard Wood; when Wood was promoted, Roosevelt was raised to colonel. The Rough Riders were made up of cowboys, some Indians, wealthy college graduates, and other eager young men.

The Rough Riders were in two battles: Kettle Hill and San Juan Hill. Roosevelt never forgot the men who had served with him. They were friends for life; even when he was president, he helped keep some of them out of jail and found jobs for them. When he returned from the war, "Teddy" Roosevelt received great attention from the public, as well as from politicians.

Tom Platt, leader of New York's Republicans, set aside his own plans and let Roosevelt run for governor. He won and began making changes that made him unpopular with party leaders. They wanted him moved out and suggested that McKinley make Roosevelt his running mate in 1900. At the Republican Convention, Roosevelt was chosen as nominee for vice president by enthusiastic delegates.

There was little for Roosevelt to do as vice president. When someone suggested that he go on a speaking tour, he thought it was a "bully" idea. He did not finish his tour; President McKinley was shot and killed. Now, as one of his critics said: "That cowboy is in the White House." He pledged to carry out McKinley's policies, knowing that almost everything McKinley had pledged to do had already been done.

ROOSEVELT AS PRESIDENT. Unlike Harrison, Cleveland, and McKinley, Theodore Roosevelt left much of the work to his cabinet. He enjoyed playing with his six children. He pushed physical exercise, and those around him learned to play tennis, hike, and ride horses. Army officers complained about having to do so much exercising; he shamed them by riding a horse 100 miles. White House dinners included a wide variety of guests, from boxers to royalty; all were greeted with equal hospitality. Decisions were made quickly. The public identified with him, and he enjoyed getting headlines. One writer said that "if Roosevelt went to a wedding, he thought he was the bride; if he went to a funeral, he thought he was the corpse."

Foreign policy was an area where Roosevelt was more free to do things his way than in domestic policy. He wanted the world to take notice of the United States and to see it as a major power to be treated with respect. The Navy had grown stronger since Arthur had been president, but it had two oceans to patrol. The idea of a canal across the isthmus between North and South America had been discussed for years, and some efforts had begun to build it. A company had tried without success to build one in Nicaragua, but the best location was Panama. The New Panama Canal Company had started work there, but it had run short on money, equipment, and workers.

Colombia owned Panama at the beginning of 1903, and the United States tried to bargain with Colombia on a price tag for rights to build the canal. When they did not agree on an amount, the people of Panama revolted against Colombia on November 3, 1903. The United States said Panama was independent on November 6 and quickly signed a treaty with Panama for a canal zone. Roosevelt later bragged: "I took the canal zone and let Congress debate, and while the debate goes on, the canal does also." The United States bought the New Panama Canal Company and took over construction. In 1906, Roosevelt went to Panama to see the progress on the canal and by doing that, became the first American president to leave the nation while in office. It was not until 1914 that the Canal opened for commercial shipping.

The British faced a new problem in the early 1900s. Germany was becoming more powerful, and the British wanted to keep the United States very friendly. One sign of this was in regard to the boundary between Alaska and Canada. To settle the boundary, the United States and Great Britain each appointed three members to a commission. By a four to two vote, the boundary was set very close to where the United States had always argued it was.

In 1904, war broke out between Russia and Japan. Most Americans sided with Japan even though the Japanese began the war with a sneak attack on the Russian fleet. The reason for disliking Russia was the cruel way its leaders were sending political prisoners to Siberia and mistreating Jews. By 1905, both sides were anxious for the war to end. Japan asked Roosevelt to work out an agreement between the two sides. He did such a good job that neither side was happy with the results. He also won the 1906 Nobel Peace Prize for his efforts.

Domestic affairs. In Congress and in his party, Roosevelt faced many who disagreed with him. They wanted to move forward at a slow, steady pace, but Roosevelt was a man of action who wanted things done right away. In this, he was in line with the thinking of Progressives. They believed that the United States was the best nation in the world, but that it could be better. They wanted a variety of things: clean government, protection of forests, an end to child labor, limits on the hours women worked, limits on alcohol consumption, and improvements in public education. Roosevelt wanted most of the same things and worked well with them.

Roosevelt loved the outdoors and traveled with his friend, Gifford Pinchot, into the woods, often taking his children along. Roosevelt set aside 150 million acres of forest lands for national use. He began to control big business. The Pure Food and Drug Act began control of food and drug sales. He enforced the Sherman Antitrust Act, and the Supreme Court broke up a big railroad combination in the Northern Securities Case in 1904.

After leaving office, Roosevelt went to Africa on safari and then to Europe. Upon returning, he clashed with President Taft, and in 1912 he ran for president on the Progressive ticket. He later clashed with President Wilson, who would not let him fight in World War I. He died in 1919.

Name: _____ Date: _____

Points to Ponder (McKinley, T. Roosevelt)

1. As a Socialist in the 1890s, who would you think should own railroads and telephones?

   _____

2. How did McKinley handle the coal miners' strike in Ohio? _____

   _____

   _____

3. What difference was there between the way McKinley and Bryan campaigned in 1896? Which was most like the way candidates campaign today?

   _____

   _____

   _____

4. Why were Americans shouting "Remember the *Maine*" in 1898?

   _____

   _____

5. How did the Spanish-American War help make Theodore Roosevelt famous?

   _____

   _____

6. How did Roosevelt shake up the New York City police department?

   _____

   _____

⭐⭐⭐ **Explore History** ⭐⭐⭐

1. Write a short biography about William Jennings Bryan and discuss his "Cross of Gold" speech; or write a report on the life of a coal miner during McKinley's presidency and the coal miners' strike.

2. Find the Panama Canal on a map and discuss the turbulent history of the construction and control of the Canal. Make a time line.

3. In 1882, Teddy Roosevelt published his first book, *The Naval War of 1812*. Name some other presidents who have had literary works published. Discuss some of their works.

4. Draw a map of the battles of the Spanish-American War.

WILLIAM HOWARD TAFT
(1857–1930, P. 1909–1913)

As Theodore Roosevelt prepared for his African safari in 1909, he exchanged pleasant words with Taft, who presented him a folding ruler to measure his kills. By 1912, the two men had become bitter enemies and ran against each other in the national election.

Taft was born in 1857, and he was so large as a child that ordinary baby clothes did not fit him. His father had been secretary of war, attorney general, and an ambassador. Much was expected of William, who was an excellent student in school and an above average baseball player. He graduated second in his class at Yale in 1878, and received a law degree from Cincinnati Law School in 1880. In 1886, he married Helen Herron, who was a determined woman intent on his climbing to the top. When he was 29, Taft was appointed as a judge of the Ohio superior court. Three years later, he was named United States solicitor general, the lawyer who argues cases before the United States Supreme Court. In 1892, he was appointed to the U.S. Circuit Court.

President McKinley chose Taft as head of the Philippine Commission, which set up civil government for the Filipinos. The Tafts greatly enjoyed this opportunity to travel, and when he was finished, everyone seemed pleased with his work. When Theodore Roosevelt wanted to appoint him to the Supreme Court, he declined after the Filipinos begged him to stay. In 1904, he was appointed secretary of war, and he became very close to the president. Mrs. Taft wanted him to be president, but Taft said politics made him sick; he preferred a seat on the Supreme Court. It took great effort on the part of Roosevelt and Mrs. Taft to convince him to run for president in 1908.

When Roosevelt announced he wanted Taft to be his replacement, no other candidates had a chance. The Democrats chose William Jennings Bryan for the third time. Bryan had run in 1896, 1900, and now in 1908. He believed his chances were better this time, but they were not. Taft beat him by 1.2 million popular votes and 321–162 in electoral votes. Bryan was finished as a presidential candidate, but he remained powerful in the Democratic Party.

Roosevelt decided it was best if he got out of Taft's way for a while, so he went on safari in Africa. Newspapers were kept informed on how many animals had been killed each day. After that, he went to Europe where he met many of the heads of state. Roosevelt grew suspicious that Germany had plans to expand. In Great Britain, he represented Taft at the funeral of King Edward VII.

TAFT AS PRESIDENT. The new president was far different from the energetic, excitable Roosevelt. Taft had always been too heavy, and he began his term weighing 250 pounds. At one point, his weight was up to 320 pounds. He was often tired and many times he fell asleep during cabinet meetings and once during a funeral in which he was sitting in the front row. An oversized bathtub was installed in the White House to accommodate him. His doctors and wife kept after him to cut down on his eating, but he sneaked into the kitchen and grabbed snacks between meals.

Taft's main exercise was golf, which many thought was a rich man's sport. He also enjoyed dancing, and in the evening, he and Mrs. Taft danced to phonograph records. He sneaked off to baseball games, and in 1910, he threw the first ball of the season, a tradition other presidents have continued. At one game, he stood during the seventh inning, and that began the tradition of the "seventh-inning stretch." The people of Tokyo sent him 3,000 Japanese cherry trees, which were planted along the Potomac River.

Taft was not good at politics. He did not greet people with the enthusiasm Roosevelt had; in fact, he often did not know their names. He had ideas about improvements that were needed but failed to get the public support he needed to accomplish them.

Speaker of the House Joe Cannon was an old conservative who did not want changes, so he stopped bills he did not like from being considered. An effort was made by a group of reformers to take away some of Cannon's powers. When Taft did not help them, the reformers were angry with him.

A bitter argument broke out between the secretary of interior and Gifford Pinchot, the chief forester of the United States. Taft settled the argument by firing Pinchot, Roosevelt's good friend. When Roosevelt returned from his trip to Africa and Europe, Pinchot was one of the first men he met with. The firing of Pinchot was one of the reasons Roosevelt believed that Taft had perhaps been a bad choice for his successor.

Taft had said he wanted a lower tariff, but a new tariff was passed that was higher than the old one. This satisfied some Republicans, but it made many of the wealthiest party members angry. Taft defended the new tariff, which made low tariff Republicans angry with him.

Taft used the Sherman Antitrust Act to break up many large trusts (big businesses controlled by a small number of board members). His efforts made even more wealthy people angry with him.

The 1912 election. By 1912, Taft was tired of being president. He might not have run at all except for his desire to keep Roosevelt from getting the nomination. By the time of the Republican Convention, Taft had all the delegate votes he needed, but Roosevelt stirred up his supporters by claiming that Taft had rigged the convention. The Roosevelt delegates left the convention and organized the Progressive Party ticket. Roosevelt called his program the "New Nationalism." Their gathering was often called the Bull Moose Convention.

The Democrats chose Woodrow Wilson, the governor of New Jersey, as their candidate. He called his program the "New Freedom," and he wanted to regulate big business. In October, Roosevelt was shot by an insane man in Milwaukee. Even though blood poured down his shirt, he stood and gave his full speech before going to the hospital; all of the candidates then stopped campaigning. Wilson easily defeated Roosevelt and Taft, who came in third.

After he left office, Taft became a law school professor and president of the American Bar Association. During World War I, Wilson made him chairman of the War Labor Board. In 1921, President Harding gave him the prize he had always wanted: he was made chief justice of the Supreme Court. He made the Court much more efficient. Each day, he walked the three miles from his home to the Court and kept his weight down to under 300 pounds. He retired from the Court because of bad health in February 1930 and died that March.

WOODROW WILSON
(1856–1924, P. 1913–1921)

Nearly every writer describes Wilson as an idealist who wanted to achieve great goals or as a man of vision who warned what would happen if those goals were not met. Wilson was not a "practical" politician willing to compromise, and he was harsh with any who objected to his plans for the future.

Wilson was born in Virginia, the son of a Presbyterian minister. His family experienced the South's suffering during and after the Civil War. In 1879, he graduated from Princeton University and then went to the University of Virginia for his law degree. He practiced law for a few years but found it dull and not very profitable. Wilson then became a history and political science student at Johns Hopkins University where he earned a Ph.D. While there, he wrote *Congressional Government,* a book critical of the way Congress made decisions through the committee process.

Wilson became a college professor at Bryn Mawr and Wesleyan, and then he returned to teach at Princeton University in 1890. He was one of the most popular teachers at the university and was known for his brilliant lectures. In 1902, he was named the university's president. He pushed for changes that would make the students more scholarly and the school more democratic. He clashed with the dean of the graduate school; when a friend reminded Wilson there were two sides to every question, he replied: "Yes, the right and the wrong." By 1910, it appeared Wilson was losing the fight and might be dismissed by the trustees.

At the same time, the New Jersey Democrats were looking for a candidate for governor. Wilson resigned as Princeton's president and campaigned hard. He was elected and pushed a number of bills through the legislature to improve local government and regulate politics and public utilities. His proposals for direct election of senators, party primaries, and election reform were made law over the objections of leaders of both political parties. Many reformers from around the country took notice. One who visited him was Franklin D. Roosevelt, a New York state senator. Another visitor was Colonel E.M. House from Texas, who began a drive in the South to support Wilson for the Democratic Party's nomination for president.

At the Democratic Convention of 1912, Wilson's main opponent was Speaker of the House Champ Clark. Wilson was nominated on the forty-sixth ballot. In the campaign, Wilson criticized Taft for being too close to "privileged big business." He called for idealism and the "rule of justice and right." He did not think a revolution was needed, but the nation needed a "new point of view and a new method..." His main advantage in the campaign was the wide-open split between Taft and Roosevelt, who spent more effort attacking each other than working against him. In the election, Wilson received 435 electoral votes, Roosevelt 88, and Taft 8. In popular votes, his two opponents had over 1 million more popular votes than he had.

WILSON AS PRESIDENT (first term). Wilson was determined to get his program through Congress, and he began using an office in the Capitol building to meet with leaders. He called

Congress into special session. Breaking with a tradition that went back to Jefferson, he appeared before a joint session and persuaded them to lower the tariff. Part of the new tariff included an income tax, now constitutional under the Sixteenth Amendment. The tax was only one percent on incomes over $3,000, and it went as high as six percent on incomes over $500,000.

Wilson next addressed the complex problem of the banking system, and in time, Congress created the Federal Reserve System. The Federal Reserve is the bank from which local banks can borrow money. It controls the rate of interest on loans; by doing that, it can raise or lower interest rates for people who borrow from banks.

The Clayton Antitrust Act made control over big business stronger. It prohibited unfair business practices. It said that labor unions were not combinations in restraint of trade and that peaceful strikes were legal. The Federal Trade Commission was created to keep an eye on business.

Foreign problems. Neither Wilson nor Secretary of State Bryan were experts in international affairs. They had no idea that the United States was going to be involved in issues around the world and would soon face the largest war the world had yet seen.

During a time of revolution in Mexico, Wilson began sending help to Venustiano Carranza, an opponent of General Victoriano Huerta, the corrupt leader of Mexico. Eventually, Carranza succeeded in overthrowing Huerta and became president. Then, Francisco Villa, who had supported Carranza, began raiding Mexico and killed 18 Americans at a mining camp. In 1916, Villa captured Columbus, New Mexico, killing 16 Americans. With Carranza's reluctant permission, Wilson sent General John J. Pershing into Mexico to capture Villa. It was like a search for a needle in a haystack, and Pershing's men finally returned home in February 1917. The failure of Pershing's effort gave Germany the impression the U.S. Army was weak, and during World War I, Germany sent secret agents into Mexico to stir up anger among the Mexican people.

World War I broke out in Europe in 1914, and one nation after another was drawn in. Many Americans were either born in Europe or had close family ties there, so they were very one-sided in their opinions of the war. However, few Americans wanted to fight in the war; while our navy was the third largest in the world, our army was one of the smallest. Wilson and Bryan favored neutrality as the proper policy to follow. In his heart, Wilson leaned toward Great Britain from the beginning.

Neither the Germans nor the British were interested in "playing fair," and they made up their own rules as the war progressed. The British started inspecting ships bound for Germany to make sure there were no war supplies on board. The United States protested, but after the British paid for goods taken from ships, most Americans were satisfied. Ships bound for European ports other than Germany were also stopped and searched.

The Germans were not as strong in surface ships as the Allies, Britain and France, so they built up a large submarine fleet to attack ships taking supplies across the Atlantic. In 1915, they warned other nations that a submarine war zone had been declared around the British Isles. Any ship flying any flag would be sunk. Ads were placed in U.S. newspapers, warning Americans of the danger of traveling on Allied ships through the war zone. In May 1915, the British-owned passenger liner *Lusitania* was sunk off the Irish coast; 1,198 people were killed, which included 128 Americans. Even though the ship was carrying war supplies and had orders to ram submarines, the attack seemed cruel.

Americans were still not ready to fight, but Wilson wrote a letter to Germany. The letter was written so strongly that Secretary Bryan feared it might bring war, and he resigned. After another ship was sunk, the Germans realized sinking ships might cause the United States to enter the war against them, so they backed off.

In 1916, the Republicans chose Charles Evans Hughes of the Supreme Court as their presidential candidate, rather than the anti-German Theodore Roosevelt. The Democrats chose Wilson again and used the slogan: "He kept us out of the war." Wilson barely won the election. If Hughes had received 3,900 more votes in California, he would have won.

WILSON AS PRESIDENT (second term). After the election, Germany began "unrestricted submarine warfare"; they would sink any ship coming close to the British Isles. Germany was gambling that Great Britain would be defeated before the United States could raise and send an army to help them. In April 1917, the United States declared war on Germany. Wilson said that it was "a war to end all wars" and was "to make the world safe for democracy."

World War I. By the time the United States entered the war, Europe had been fighting for three years. The war was not going well when the United States entered it. Great Britain had only a six-week supply of food on hand in the spring of 1917. The French army faced mutinies by soldiers who refused to fight any more. Czarist Russia had experienced a revolution, and then its government was overthrown by the Communists, led by Lenin.

The first priority was to stop the German submarines. The Allies started sending convoys across the Atlantic protected by fast destroyers. The system worked well, and by the end of the war, submarines were far less dangerous for ships than before.

The United States began a quick increase in the number of soldiers. By the end of the war, two million had volunteered and two million others had been drafted. Large camps were built to train them quickly, and the government had to supply them with food, clothing, and rifles in enormous numbers. The nation's factories were running at full speed, with the War Labor Board under former President Taft making sure labor strikes did not slow production. Railroads were temporarily taken over by the government to make sure trains got the supplies where they were needed. American civilians were encouraged to help in the war effort as well. Children worked in "liberty gardens" to grow vegetables, and adults bought "liberty bonds" to help pay for the war. Speakers were sent to explain why the United States was in the war.

The U.S. Army sent to fight the war was called the A.E.F. (American Expeditionary Force), and it was led by General John J. Pershing. The first 80,000 American troops arrived in March 1918, and another 663,000 arrived by the end of June. By the fall of 1918, Germans wanted to end the war, but Wilson told them that he would never make peace as long as their ruler, Kaiser Wilhelm II, ruled. After some major battles, the Germans realized they could not win, the Kaiser resigned, and Germany signed an armistice (a temporary agreement to stop fighting) on November 11, 1918.

The peace conference. In January 1918, Wilson announced the Fourteen Points, his goals for the war. The Fourteenth Point was the creation of a "general association of nations" to protect the peace in the future. Instead of sending someone to represent him, Wilson went to the peace conference at Versailles (the royal estate near Paris) himself. There he met with other world leaders; while he worked out details for a "League of Nations" to debate issues rather than fight, other leaders decided other matters. Germany complained about some parts of the treaty, but they were forced to sign or face Allied armies invading their country.

When Wilson brought the League covenant (constitution) home with him, it met strong opposition from Senate leaders. After long hearings and debates, they turned down the treaty and the League. Wilson tried to fight for his League; however, he suffered a stroke and became paralyzed. His dream failed for the time being, but it came back to life later in the United Nations Charter.

Name: _____ Date: _____

Points to Ponder (Taft, Wilson)

1. Why did Taft turn down Roosevelt's offer of a seat on the Supreme Court?

   _____

   _____

   _____

2. After Taft was inaugurated, what did Roosevelt do to get out of his way?

   _____

   _____

   _____

3. What baseball traditions did Taft start?

   _____

   _____

   _____

   _____

4. What problem was created by Taft's firing of Pinchot?

   _____

   _____

   _____

   _____

5. What job did President Harding give Taft that he had always wanted?

   _____

   _____

6. How did Wilson's years as a boy cause him to fear war?

   _____

   _____

   _____

   _____

   _____

Points to Ponder (Taft, Wilson)

7. How did Wilson feel about compromising?

    _____

    _____

    _____

8. As president, what did Wilson do about the tariff and banking?

    _____

    _____

    _____

9. Why did Germany sign the treaty when they thought it was unfair?

    _____

    _____

    _____

10. What happened to the treaty in the Senate? What later grew out of the idea of a "general association of nations"?

    _____

    _____

    _____

    _____

    _____

☆ ☆ ☆ **Explore History** ☆ ☆ ☆

1. Write a report about Gifford Pinchot and his involvement with conservation and forestry. How do you think his ideas were similar to that of conservationists today?

2. Make a diorama or a poster about things Americans on the homefront did to help the war effort, such as liberty bonds and gardens, the collection of scrap metal, and so on. Find copies of some advertising of the time that promoted the war effort.

3. Imagine that you were related to someone who died on the *Lusitania.* Compose an editorial to your newspaper or write a letter to President Wilson, expressing your feelings regarding the incident.

4. Write a short biography about Joseph "Uncle Joe" Cannon.

WARREN HARDING
(1865-1923, P. 1921-1923)

It is important to have friends, but a person needs friends who will help him, not hurt him. The problem for Warren Harding was he did not choose the right friends. By the time they were finished, his "friends" had destroyed his reputation as well as his will to live.

Harding was born in Ohio in 1865; his father was a farmer who studied medicine and became a doctor when Warren was eight years old. Mr. Harding liked to invest in businesses, one of which was a newspaper. When Warren was six years old, he started running errands for the work-ers. He also worked on his father's farm, but he liked living in town better. Warren was an average student in school, and his mother wanted him to be a minister. He went to Ohio Central College, but he made only average grades; he was much more interested in playing in the band and editing the yearbook than studying.

Harding taught for one semester after he left college, but he decided "it was the hardest job I ever had" and quit. By this time, his family had moved to Marion, Ohio. The newspaper, the Marion *Star,* was for sale for only $300 and the payment of its debts. He bought it, and after a few years Marion grew and the *Star* began to show a profit. Marion was a Republican town in a Democratic county, so Harding had to be careful about how he approached politics. Since he was a Republican, he usually said nicer things about the Republicans than the Democrats.

Harding married Florence Kling, the daughter of a prominent Marion family, in 1891. Her father was furious, and it took 15 years for him to make peace with his son-in-law. After they married, Florence went down to the newspaper and started running the business. She was much better at running the paper than her husband was. Harding gave raises to his employees behind her back, played poker with them, and won most of it back.

In 1898, Harding was elected to the state senate and was soon the most popular member. He loved people, and the voters loved him. He met Harry Daugherty, a man wise in politics, who took him up the ladder to success. In 1902, Harding became lieutenant governor, but he lost twice in his race for the governor's job. In 1914, he was elected to the U.S. Senate. He loved the Senate but not the work. He just enjoyed the conversations, the golf courses, the race tracks, and the ball parks. He was everyone's friend. When a bill came up, he voted the way he thought the people back home wanted. He was especially kind to business, and he either voted for what business wanted or did not vote if it might offend the people back home.

In 1920, Harding ran for the Senate and the presidency at the same time. He did not think he would get the nomination for president, but Daugherty did. Daugherty believed none of the favored candidates would get enough delegate votes to win, and in frustration, they would turn to Harding. His prediction came true. Harding was chosen by the party convention, even though many delegates did not know who he was. For vice president, the delegates chose Governor Calvin Coolidge of Massachusetts.

The Democrats chose Governor James Cox of Ohio for president and Franklin D. Roosevelt of New York for vice president. The 1920 election was almost over before the first person voted.

Harding won, not because of his brilliant program, but because voters were so angry with Woodrow Wilson and the Democrats. They did not trust his League of Nations, and many were suffering from high unemployment, high prices, and wartime government regulations. They wanted to get their lives back to normal.

Harding was ideal. He stressed small town values and leaving people alone. He was easygoing, and not very moral. There were rumors about love affairs and his violations of prohibition laws. His speeches soothed the voters. He said what America needed was "not heroics but healing, not nostrums [cures] but normalcy."

Harding won by a landslide. He received a record seven million more votes than Cox, and beat him 404–127 in electoral votes.

HARDING AS PRESIDENT. A key to the success or failure of any president is the people appointed to high positions. Party leaders chose some of these for Harding: Charles Evans Hughes as secretary of state, Andrew Mellon as secretary of the treasury, and Herbert Hoover as secretary of commerce. Harding chose former President Taft for the Supreme Court. All of these men did their jobs well, and Harding did not interfere with their work. The steps forward during his three years as president were the result of their efforts. The Washington Naval Conference was led by Hughes, and it put limits on the numbers of battleships. Mellon put the government on a budget for the first time and pushed for tax reductions. Hoover encouraged business growth.

Harding had the courage to release Eugene Debs from prison for violating a wartime law. After freeing him, he invited Debs to the White House. Debs was a Socialist and very unpopular with most Republicans, but Harding thought it was the right thing to do.

Unfortunately, Harding also gave jobs to some of his friends, and they took advantage of him. His friend Harry Daugherty was made attorney general, and he took bribes. Charles Forbes was put in charge of the Veterans Bureau; he and his friends got rich by selling sheets and towels from veterans' hospitals. Harding's poker friend Albert Fall became secretary of the

interior. He worked out a scheme to sell oil from government oil reserves set aside for the navy. It was not until 1924 that the details of this story were made known to the public as the Teapot Dome Scandal.

Harding was sick with worry that all these things would be exposed. He went west for a vacation and died unexpectedly in California in 1923. After his death, people found out about the scandals, and his memory was disgraced. His death made Calvin Coolidge the next president.

CALVIN COOLIDGE
(1872–1933, P. 1923–1929)

Vice President Calvin Coolidge was on vacation in Vermont when he was notified that President Harding was dead. His father, a justice of the peace, gave him the oath of office as president. When he arrived in Washington, the oath was admininistered again by a Supreme Court justice.

Coolidge was born in Plymouth, Vermont, a small town where his father ran a country store. The men of small New England communities often gathered around the cracker barrel of such stores and discussed politics. John Coolidge was often involved in local and state politics; he was town constable for many years and was a member of the state legislature. After attending the local school and an academy, Calvin attended Amherst College. He got off to a slow start in college, but graduated near the top of his class. He had already developed his sense of humor. One day, hash was served at the boarding house where he ate his meals. He looked at the hash, asked the waiter to bring the cat in, was then satisfied, and ate the hash.

After graduating, Coolidge moved to Massachusetts where he studied law for two years, then he opened his law practice. He served in many local offices: city council, city attorney, county clerk of the courts, the state legislature, mayor, state senator, lieutenant governor, and governor. He married Grace Goodhue in 1905; she was outgoing and cheerful; he was shy and serious, but hardworking. He once said: "Let men in public office substitute the light that comes from the midnight oil for the limelight." They were a devoted couple, at their best when they were together.

Governor Coolidge became noted for efficiency. He reorganized the state executive offices and was the first governor to offer an executive budget for the legislature to consider. The event that gave him a reputation beyond Massachusetts was the Boston Police Strike in 1919. A dispute had broken out between the police and the police commissioner when they voted to join the AFL labor union. The commissioner fired 19 policemen who had joined, and the police force went out on strike. That night, there were riots and lootings in the city. The mayor called out some of the National Guard, but Coolidge was reluctant to call in more guardsmen. When the AFL president protested, Coolidge sent him a telegram: "There is no right to strike against the public safety by anybody, anywhere, any time." Coolidge was now a hero to many Americans who were fearful that the radicals were taking over.

At the Republican Convention of 1920, Harding was chosen for president by the party leaders, and the other delegates went along. When the leaders chose a candidate for vice president, the delegates rebelled and chose Coolidge. When he told his wife he had been nominated, she asked: "You aren't going to take it, are you?" He said: "I suppose I shall have to."

After Harding's landslide victory, the Coolidges moved to Washington and lived in a hotel, as they had done when he was governor. President Harding invited him to sit in on cabinet meetings, but he said little. He presided over the Senate as the Constitution provides, but did not try to draw attention to himself. Whatever rumors and suspicions he heard about Harding, he kept to himself.

As vice president, Coolidge was invited to many dinners, and he always accepted. At one, the host wondered why he came when he did not seem to enjoy himself. Coolidge said: "Got to eat somewhere."

COOLIDGE AS PRESIDENT. Coolidge kept Harding's cabinet without change, but he relied mostly on Hoover and Mellon for advice. The new president had no major policy changes to make in economic matters. He said: "The business of America is business" and promoted business growth. Business had expanded beyond anyone's dreams. The automobile had gone from a wealthy man's toy to a common sight on the street. The movie industry had become a major source of entertainment, as had the radio program. Travel had become so large that streets and roads had to be improved. Department stores and grocery chains had developed.

Another large industry that had grown was the illegal sale of alcohol in violation of the Eighteenth Amendment and the Volstead Act. J. Edgar Hoover was appointed director of the FBI in 1924, and he began a crackdown on this business. Other than prohibition violation, business was encouraged.

Coolidge supported reduction of the national debt and cutting government expenses. He opposed sending relief after a terrible flood hit Mississippi until a study of the damage had been finished.

Coolidge had not been president long before the rumors about Harding's presidency were being openly discussed. A book was published on *The Strange Death of President Harding,* which said Mrs. Harding had poisoned her husband. Even more serious were charges that during the Harding presidency, illegal deals were made by Secretary of Interior Albert Fall to lease government oil reserves at Teapot Dome, Wyoming, and Elks Hill, California, to two rich oil men. It was eventually discovered that bribes had been made. Former Secretary Fall was sentenced to a year in prison. Attorney General Daugherty had also received bribes, and he was fired.

The election of 1924. The Democrats were so divided in 1924 they had a hard time picking a candidate. Eastern Democrats favored Governor Al Smith of New York, but Southern and western Democrats did not like him because he was Catholic. On the 103rd ballot, they compromised on John W. Davis, a wealthy New Yorker. Coolidge won 382–136 in electoral votes. Robert LaFollette, the Progressive party candidate, carried only his home state of Wisconsin. The nation was assured another four years of "Coolidge prosperity."

Coolidge is best known for his refusal to use more words than necessary. One woman asked what his hobby was, and he answered: "Holding office." Another said she had bet a friend she could get him to say three words, and he answered: "You lose." In 1927, he said: "I do not choose to run for president in 1928." A new leader was waiting in the wings.

Name: _____ Date: _____

Points to Ponder (Harding, Coolidge)

1. What did Harding like most about being in politics? What interest group did he usually support?

   _____

   _____

   _____

2. How did cabinet members like Hughes, Mellon, and Hoover give the impression the government was doing fine? How did Harding help them?

   _____

   _____

   _____

3. What would you say was the reason Harding failed as president?

   _____

   _____

4. How did Coolidge become nationally famous? _____

   _____

   _____

5. Coolidge reduced the national debt and lowered taxes. How was he able to do both at the same time?

   _____

   _____

⭐ ⭐ ⭐ **Explore History** ⭐ ⭐ ⭐

1. Write a mini-report on the Teapot Dome Scandal and Secretary of the Interior Albert Fall.

2. Design a travel brochure for tourists, listing some places of interest in the United States, such as Mount Rushmore or Hoover Dam. Include a brief history and pictures of each place you choose.

3. Make a poster to show the growing businesses that were changing America during the Coolidge administration.

4. Write an interview with J. Edgar Hoover about his crackdown on the illegal manufacture and sale of alcohol.

HERBERT HOOVER
(1874–1964, P. 1929–1933)

No one was ever elected president by more people and yet rejected by more people when he ran for a second term than was Herbert Clark Hoover. The reason for his decline in popularity was the Great Depression. A few predicted it was coming, but none could have predicted its terrible effect, not only on the United States, but on other nations as well. The blame fell on Hoover, whether he deserved the blame or not.

Hoover was born in West Branch, Iowa, in 1874. His father died when he was six, and his mother died when he was eight. He was taken in by Quaker relatives in Oregon, who taught him the importance of hard work and service. He enrolled in the new Stanford University in California in 1891; it was there that he met Lou Henry, who later became his wife. He was an excellent engineering student, and she was a geology student. After graduating, he went to Australia where he developed a new system for gold mining. He was then hired as chief engineer for a Chinese mining company. He married Lou in 1898, and the trip to China became their honeymoon. They often worked together; when she could not go, she studied Chinese with a tutor. Hoover discovered major coal deposits in northwest China. While the Hoovers were there, an anti-foreigner group called the Boxers attacked anyone who was not Chinese. In Peking, where he and other foreigners lived, they were in great danger. Hoover organized the men, while his wife organized the women for defense.

Hoover's success took him to a major mining company in England. His job took him around the world many times, and he was perhaps as well-traveled as any American of his time. When World War I came, he took charge of relief work in Belgium. People began referring to him as the "Great Humanitarian." President Wilson appointed him food administrator during the war. After the war, he went to Europe to prevent people from starving in Germany and Austria. Both political parties wanted him to run on their ticket, but Hoover took the position of secretary of commerce under Presidents Harding and Coolidge.

As secretary of commerce, Hoover's constant theme was that government should help business, not get into it. He wrote pamphlets encouraging the citizen to save his money and be self-reliant and hardworking. The Commerce Department became the most efficient in the government. In 1928, when it was clear Coolidge did not want another term, the spotlight was on Hoover, and he easily won the Republican nomination.

The election of 1928. The Democrats chose as their candidate the same man they had rejected in 1924, Governor Al Smith of New York. Smith was still Catholic and still "wet" (favoring an end to prohibition); those became the great issues of the campaign. Many Americans feared that a Catholic president would let the Pope take over. As ridiculous as it seems today, there were rumors that Smith planned to build a tunnel under the Atlantic to the Vatican. The Ku Klux Klan was not only attacking African-Americans, but Catholics as well. They were very powerful at the time.

Hoover did not discuss the religion issue, but he called prohibition a "noble experiment." His party's main theme was prosperity, and some Republicans used the phrase: "a chicken in every pot and two cars in every garage." Hoover himself said: "We in America today are nearer to the final triumph over poverty than ever before in the history of the land." Those words came back to haunt him later.

The election was another landslide: Hoover won 444–87 in electoral votes and 21.3 million to 15 million in popular votes. In accounting for his victory, Hoover said: "General prosperity was on my side."

HOOVER AS PRESIDENT. Hoover had been in office six months when the stock market started dropping at alarming rates. On October 29, 1929, the bottom fell out. There were no buyers, and stocks were being sold for practically nothing. *Variety,* the show business newspaper, put it best: "Wall Street Lays an Egg." Hoover began calling conferences of business leaders to encourage them. He gave statements saying that the problem was only temporary and that business would return to normal in weeks.

Hoover urged business to increase production and hire more workers; he talked to states about new building projects. It did no good. Business was afraid the situation would get worse, and state tax revenues were dropping. Hoover hoped to encourage spending by cutting federal taxes, but the taxes were already so low that it did no good.

Everything began falling apart. "A" lost money on the stock market, so he cancelled the order for a new car from "B." With car sales falling, "C" fired "B," and at the factory, "D" lost his assembly line job because sales were so weak. "D" could no longer afford his house payments and had to move into rental property. The price of everything was falling, and banks were in trouble because they had lent money to "A," "B," "C," "D," and many more. Bank deposits were not protected, so those with money in the bank started taking their money out. Banks began to close. People who had money did not want to spend it, fearing they might lose their jobs.

Hoover did not believe in the federal government giving relief; that was the job of charities and states. He did try other strategies. He urged farmers to cut crop production, but fearing the bank might take their land, farmers produced more. He tried lending money to banks, railroads, and other large businesses through the RFC (Reconstruction Finance Corporation); that failed, however. Hoover was also very concerned about keeping the budget balanced, but many Americans felt it was more important to take care of the unemployed and the needy.

The Depression was also destroying other countries, and in some, the people were turning to radicals for solutions. In Germany, Hitler came to power, and in Japan, the military replaced the civilian government.

FRANKLIN D. ROOSEVELT
(1882–1945, P. 1933–1945)

No president ever held office during a time with such a variety of crucial events than did Franklin Roosevelt. Those who loved him said he had not only saved the nation but the world as well. Those who hated him called him a charlatan and trickster whose "reign" had destroyed the balance of federal and state governments, had created the "welfare state," and had forced the United States into World War II. One thing was certain: the American public's feelings about him were never neutral.

FDR, as he came to be called later, was born into a wealthy family residing at Hyde Park, New York. His father had made his fortune in coal, shipping, and railroads. He was the only child, and his mother was overly-protective. She wanted him to have the best of everything. His fifth cousin, Theodore Roosevelt, was a Republican, but he had a close tie to Franklin's father, James, a loyal Democrat. Franklin attended Groton Academy, a school for very wealthy boys, where he began to show concern for the less fortunate. In 1900, he entered Harvard, where he got by with a "C" average but earned his degree in three years. While he was at Harvard, he fell in love with Eleanor Roosevelt, a distant cousin who was Theodore's niece. After graduating from Harvard, he married Eleanor in 1905. After a year at Columbia University Law School, he became a lawyer.

Eleanor was an unusual person. She was born into a wealthy family, but she never cared much for wealth or position. She had been very shy as a girl and was so old-fashioned that her nickname was "Granny." Eleanor changed over the years into a dynamic woman with the ability to meet a leader as well as a common person and to make both feel welcome. By the end of her life, people were calling her "First Lady of the World."

In 1910, Franklin was elected to the state senate, and in 1912 he campaigned hard for Woodrow Wilson, whom he greatly admired. Wilson appointed him assistant secretary of the navy, where he learned much about national defense and foreign policy. In 1920, FDR ran with James M. Cox as the vice presidential candidate; he and Cox were beaten in a Republican landslide.

In 1921, Roosevelt contracted polio; his legs were paralyzed, and he was in great pain. By hard work and determination, he was able to walk again within a year with the aid of heavy braces. He built up his upper body to compensate for the weakness of his lower body. He began going down to Warm Springs, Georgia, to swim and strengthen his legs. During the next three years, Eleanor kept him involved in politics and his law career.

Al Smith asked him to take charge of his 1924 presidential campaign. When he slowly walked across the stage to give his speech at the Democratic convention, the delegates knew how much courage he had shown and gave him a long standing ovation. Roosevelt called Smith "the happy warrior." Smith did not get the nomination, but FDR was on his way. In 1928, FDR again led the Smith campaign, and FDR ran for governor; Smith lost, FDR won.

New York was hard hit by the Depression, and FDR pushed a number of programs to help the poor and unemployed. To pay for the programs, income taxes were raised on the wealthy. In 1932, FDR was running for president, and so were three others, including Al Smith. FDR argued that it was time for the federal government to come to the aid of the poor. To win, he offered the vice president position to John Nance Garner, the favorite son of Texas. After being nominated, FDR flew to Chicago to address the convention, the first time that had been done by any candidate. He told them: "I pledge you, I pledge myself, to a new deal for the American people." The "New Deal" became the name for his program.

The campaign of 1932. FDR loved to campaign and gave 16 major speeches, each devoted to one topic. His attacks on the Depression made Hoover angry, so he started campaigning. Hoover argued that the Depression had been caused by worldwide collapse, and Democrats in Congress had refused to cooperate with him in finding answers. When the people voted, FDR won by over seven million popular votes and 472–59 in electoral votes. It was clear that the nation wanted a new deal.

ROOSEVELT AS PRESIDENT (first term). By March 1933, when FDR became president, one of every four Americans was unemployed, 5,504 banks had closed, and many farmers were losing their land because they could not pay their mortgages. A few thousand veterans had marched on Washington demanding their pensions immediately, and they had been driven out of town by soldiers with tanks. Many people were traveling across the nation looking for jobs. FDR assured the nation in his inaugural address that "The only thing we have to fear is fear itself." He proposed new programs, and Congress quickly approved them in what came to be known as the "Hundred Days."

FDR began with the banking crisis. All banks were closed until their books could be examined to decide which were strong enough to survive. FDR went on the radio with his first "Fireside Chat" to assure people that when their bank reopened, their money would be safe. The people believed him, and more deposited their money than withdrew it. To protect bank accounts, the Federal Deposit Insurance Corporation (FDIC) was created to insure them, and bank runs, in which everyone wanted to withdraw his or her money at the same time, became a thing of the past.

To save money, FDR cut the salaries of federal workers and veterans' pensions. Another group of veterans came to Washington. Instead of driving them out, he sent hot coffee to them. A group of veterans met with one of his assistants, and then they all went home.

New spending programs came one after another. The Civilian Conservation Corps (CCC) was created to employ young men in work projects. They lived in barracks and received $25 a month, one-half of which went to their families. They received good food, an education, hard work, and fresh air. The Federal Emergency Relief Administration (FERA) gave states money for relief programs.

Farmers had been hurt by too much production, and that had cut prices they received for their products. A new program, the Agricultural Adjustment Act, was created to pay farmers to take land out of production. Crops in the ground were plowed under; six million pigs were slaughtered and their bodies ground up and buried. Farm prices went up. Some said it was because of the AAA; others said it happened because of droughts in farm areas.

Another program that caused much debate was the National Recovery Administration (NRA). Instead of punishing businesses for setting prices, it called for meetings of industries to set prices. If the price of $1 was set for a widget, then all widget manufacturers had to charge $1 for it. Codes set wages for an industry as well. If the wage for a skilled widget maker was set at 40¢ an hour, that was the wage all skilled widget makers were paid. The labor codes abolished child labor.

Electric service had been slow to reach much of the South. The Tennessee Valley Authority (TVA) was created to build dams along the Tennessee River for flood control and to provide electric power. However, the farms and homes of thousands of people were in that area, so they had to sell their land and move because their homes would have soon been under water.

In 1934, the Securities and Exchange Commission (SEC) was created to correct problems in the stock market. Any business selling stocks now had to provide accurate information on the company. The Federal Communications Commission (FCC) regulated the communications industry: radio stations, telephone, and telegraph.

Government was now regulating economic areas it had never touched before, and while FDR remained popular, there were critics who did not like what was happening. The rich were so unhappy they were calling FDR "that man." But there were others who said he was not doing enough. One of these, Senator Huey Long of Louisiana, called for a much heavier tax on the rich. Dr. Francis Townsend, a doctor who found himself poor at the age of 66, developed a program to help the elderly; it would give every person "of good character" over the age of 60 $200 per month, provided he spent every penny of it by the next payday.

The Supreme Court was also critical of some New Deal programs. The Court declared the NRA unconstitutional in 1935. Part of the AAA was ruled unconstitutional in 1936, and the second AAA was created to avoid the mistakes of the first one. FDR was angry with the Court for its criticism, and he referred to the Court as "the nine old men."

FDR felt the pressure for even more changes. The Works Progress Administration (WPA) was created to give jobs to all kinds of people, from the very skilled to the unskilled. Most of its money went to street and road projects, public buildings, and parks. The Rural Electrification Administration (REA) brought electric power to rural areas. Social Security came in 1935 as an insurance program to help those over 65 years of age, the blind, and crippled children.

The election of 1936. By 1936, few Republicans held any high offices. Republicans were outnumbered in the House 103 to 319 and in the Senate 25 to 69. The Republican candidate for president was Governor Alf Landon of Kansas; the only question was how badly the Republicans would lose. When the results were in, Roosevelt won 523–8 in the electoral vote and by over 11 million popular votes. The new Congress was even more Democratic.

The Supreme Court battle. FDR was feeling great, and he now made one of the few serious political mistakes of his career. He planned to add up to six more members to the Supreme Court. It took little time for Congress to react against the president, and the public was outraged as well. Chief Justice Hughes sent a letter to Congress saying that the Court was up-to-date with the cases before it and adding more justices would only slow it down. FDR's proposal went down in flaming defeat in Congress. Some changes were made in lower courts, but the Supreme Court remained untouched. Within months, two Supreme Court justices retired and two died; the whole fight had been unnecessary. Roosevelt could now appoint justices more favorable to his policies.

New programs. There was a rise in unemployment in 1937, and a new agency, the Public Works Administration (PWA), began new building projects in nearly every U.S. county. By 1939, it had spent $6 billion.

Rising discontent with FDR. By 1938, FDR had more critics than ever before, and the public elected 79 more Republicans to the House and eight to the Senate. Just as serious to FDR was the rebellion of southern Democrats in Congress, who joined with Republicans to block his more liberal programs. The New Deal period had ended. FDR supporters said he had changed the United States from a land without hope to a thriving nation again. The critics said he had wasted billions of dollars in work and relief programs, and had made government too important.

World War II. Had it not been for a new world crisis, the story of FDR might have ended in 1940, but the new war threat extended his administration. Many countries in the world were dictatorships in the 1930s. Communists had taken control of the Soviet Union, and Fascists had ruled Italy since the 1920s. Germany was in the hands of Hitler's Nazis in 1933 and began its attacks on Jews two years later. In 1931, the Japanese invaded Manchuria, taking it from the Chinese. When the League of Nations criticized Japan, it left the League.

Americans began to worry that another war was imminent. They tried to avoid it by passing laws that would deter citizens from traveling on the ships of nations at war and by putting an embargo (a refusal to sell) on nations at war. FDR was not in favor of these laws, but he could not stop them from being passed.

In 1935, a series of actions took place as dictators began grabbing land. The Italians, led by Mussolini, attacked Ethiopia, one of the few independent countries in Africa. The Spanish Civil War began in 1936, with Germany helping one side and the Russians helping the other. That same year, Germany took the Rhineland from France. The Japanese started bombing Shanghai, China, in 1937. In 1938, Germany took Austria and a region called the Sudeten from Czechoslovakia. In March of 1939, Germany took the rest of Czechoslovakia and invaded Poland in September 1939. Great Britain and France declared war on Germany. World War II had begun. Nothing happened until 1940, when Hitler attacked Norway, Denmark, Holland, and France.

The United States was alarmed, but opinion was divided regarding war strategy. Americans wanted to stay out of the war, but was it best to do it by building up military strength or by showing peaceful intentions by not doing anything? The United States began a "cash and carry" policy; if a nation at war wanted supplies, it could pay for them and carry them home in their own ships. However, along with this came the problem of the sinking of ships by German submarines. Prime Minister Churchill said he had nothing to offer England but "blood, toil, sweat, and tears." When German dive bombers started attacking London in "the blitz," the United States realized its own defenses were too weak.

By September 1940, the U.S. defense budget had reached $13 billion, and even though it was an election year, taxes were raised. The first peacetime draft came in 1940, and about 800,000 men were drafted in one year. State National Guards had also been called into active service. The United States sent 50 old destroyers to England to protect convoys crossing the

Atlantic. The United States began the lend-lease program in 1941 to send supplies to friendly nations at war.

In September 1941, Germany attacked the Soviet Union in an effort to reach its oil fields in the Crimea. The attack was slowed by rain, then snow; the Russians held a line from Leningrad in the north to Moscow to Stalingrad in the south.

The election of 1940. FDR ran for a third term, and a nation that felt it needed experience rather than change voted for him.

The United States enters the War. U.S. naval ships were escorting convoys across the Atlantic, and the United States sent needed supplies to China before it entered the war officially. On December 7, 1941, without warning, the Japanese attacked Pearl Harbor. The next day the United States declared war on Japan, and on December 11, the United States declared war on Germany and Italy.

The war years were very busy for the Roosevelts. The war was very complicated, and it involved civilian and military efforts. Congress cooperated and voted money for many projects they did not understand. One of these projects was the allocation of millions of dollars for the atomic bomb project without even knowing it existed. Mrs. Roosevelt traveled to military bases and sent reports to FDR. In 1941, FDR addressed the nation in what is known as the Four Freedoms Speech. This speech listed the four principles he considered essential for world peace: freedom of speech, freedom of religion, freedom from want, and freedom from fear. He made the speech to encourage Americans to support those who were fighting in WWII. The president traveled secretly to meetings of Allied leaders in Casablanca, Cairo, and Yalta. Of the three, the trip to Yalta was the most demanding for FDR. It occurred in February 1945 after he had won the 1944 election. Josef Stalin, the Russian leader, was difficult to deal with at Yalta. The president reported back to Congress when he returned from Yalta and then went to Warm Springs, Georgia, to rest. He died April 12, 1945, weeks before the war against Germany ended and four months before Japan's surrender.

Points to Ponder (Hoover, F. Roosevelt)

1. How did Hoover get the nicknames of "the great engineer" and the "great humanitarian"?

   _____

   _____

   _____

   _____

2. How did Hoover account for his success in the 1928 election?

   _____

   _____

   _____

   _____

3. How did Hoover first try to meet the crisis after the stock market collapse?

   _____

   _____

   _____

   _____

   _____

4. How did FDR get his job as assistant secretary of the navy?

   _____

   _____

   _____

   _____

5. What was the United States like when FDR took office?

   _____

   _____

   _____

   _____

   _____

Name: _____ Date: _____

Points to Ponder (Hoover, F. Roosevelt)

6. What did FDR do to improve farm income? How would you have felt about it if you had been unemployed and living in a city at the time?

_____

_____

_____

_____

7. What ended the New Deal period in 1938? _____

_____

8. What was FDR's 1941 Four Freedoms Speech about? Why did he give the speech?

_____

_____

_____

_____

9. What happened December 7, 1941? How did the United States respond?

_____

_____

_____

10. Where did FDR travel to meet world leaders? Which leader gave him the most trouble?

_____

_____

★ ★ ★ **Explore History** ★ ★ ★

1. Interview someone who lived through the Great Depression. What are some of the things we take for granted that weren't available during that time? Share your findings with the class.

2. Write a report on the Boxer Rebellion in China. How was Hoover involved?

3. Research polio. Write a report about the symptoms, treatment, and the polio vaccine.

4. Make a poster or chart about the New Deal. List the programs, such as the SEC, FDIC, AAA, REA, and so on. What were their purposes and benefits to Americans?

5. Stage a "Fireside Chat" such as FDR broadcast to the people of America. Why did these chats mean so much to Americans?

HARRY S TRUMAN
(1884–1972, P. 1945–1953)

The nation was focused on the death of FDR in the days following April 12, 1945, and Americans had tears in their eyes as the caisson slowly moved his body down Pennsylvania Avenue for the last time. After FDR's death, Harry Truman had called on Mrs. Roosevelt and asked what he could do for her. She said: "Is there anything we can do for you? For you're the one in trouble now."

Few believed Truman was up to the tasks ahead. He had neither the formal education nor the background in international affairs most felt was needed for the job. FDR had not told him about many of the problems the world and nation faced. Truman had never met such clever and experienced leaders as Churchill and Stalin. His military background was limited to his days in the National Guard and field artillery in World War I. Worse, it was a well-known fact that he had been part of a corrupt political machine, and he was some- times called "the Senator from Pendergast" behind his back. His abilities and determination had not been discovered yet.

Harry Truman was born in Lamar, Missouri, in 1884. As a boy, his poor eyesight and thick glasses made it impossible for him to play sports, so he read instead, and he especially liked history. The family moved to Independence, Missouri, when he was six years old. By the time he was 14, he had read every book in the Independence Public Library. He dreamed of going to West Point, but his eyesight kept him out. His father's financial problems made it impossible for him to attend college. After working in the Kansas City area, he returned to the farm. In August 1917, his National Guard unit was called up, and he was sent to France as a first lieutenant. His unit, Battery D, was in some of the worst fighting. He left the army as a captain. He married Bess Wallace, his childhood girlfriend, seven weeks after returning from the war.

Truman and a Jewish friend, Ed Jacobson, opened a men's clothing store in Kansas City. Business was good at first, but the hard times of 1921–1922 forced the store to close. Truman worked years to pay off its debts.

Before the store closed, Jim Pendergast, whom Truman had known in France, came in to shop. They talked, and Jim introduced Truman to his uncle, Boss Tom Pendergast, who ran politics in Kansas City and Jackson County. With Pendergast's help, Truman was elected a county judge (commissioner) and proved more honest and independent than anyone could have imagined. His only election loss came in 1926 when the Ku Klux Klan opposed him because he used Irish Catholic workers on county projects. He was elected to the Senate in 1934, where he supported New Deal programs. After he was re-elected in 1940, he began hearing about waste and corruption in the building of military camps. The Truman Committee was created to watch for waste, and it saved taxpayers billions of dollars.

In 1944, Vice President Henry Wallace was very unpopular, and FDR was pressured into choosing a new running mate. The person chosen was Truman, who had made no effort to get the job. His vice presidency lasted less than five weeks. When he was informed that FDR had died, he asked friends to pray for him. He told the press it felt "like the moon, the stars, and all the planets had fallen on me."

TRUMAN AS PRESIDENT. Events were moving at lightning speed, and Truman reacted quickly to them. The war was coming to an end, and the meeting to form the United Nations was to be held later that month. Germany surrendered on May 7, 1945, and Truman met at Potsdam, Germany, with Stalin and Churchill in July. Big issues faced the leaders as to what would happen to the small nations of Eastern Europe. Little was accomplished because Stalin wanted to make the region Communist.

Truman was not told about the atomic bomb project until after he became president. He appointed a committee to study the moral and military issues involved in using the bomb, but he made the final decision to use the bombs. The cities destroyed by the bombs were Hiroshima and Nagasaki; the Japanese surrendered five days after the bomb fell on Nagasaki.

The end of World War II was the beginning of Truman's struggles with Congress. He proposed a number of New Deal-type programs including federal aid to education, an increase in the minimum wage, medical insurance, and civil rights laws. He wanted to continue the Office of Price Administration (OPA) that had kept prices under control during the war. Business was anxious to return to setting its own prices, however, so it was holding back products until controls were dropped. OPA ended in 1946, and prices rose faster than wages.

Labor unions began striking for higher wages, the most critical being strikes by the coal miners and railway unions. Truman threatened to draft striking railway workers into the army and make them run the trains; the strike ended before he could carry out the threat. Coal miners ignored a court order not to strike. The union was fined $3.5 million, and its leader, John L. Lewis, was personally fined $10,000. Truman prepared to make a radio appeal to miners to return to work, but Lewis gave in, ending the strike. However, Truman's handling of the situation made him unpopular with unions.

In the 1946 elections, Republicans gained control of both Houses of Congress. They passed the Taft-Hartley Labor Law, which said a person did not have to join a union to work, permitted employers to sue unions for breach of contract, and required a 60-day waiting period before a strike could take place. The law passed over Truman's veto.

Truman was unable to accomplish much concerning domestic programs at this time, but he found Congress was willing to work with him on world problems. Senator Arthur Vandenberg, chairman of the Senate Foreign Relations Committee, convinced other Republicans to support Truman's programs to stop Communist expansion. The most important of these were the Truman Doctrine, which provided aid to Greece and Turkey to stop the spread of Communism in that region, and the Marshall Plan to rebuild Europe's economy.

The defense of the United States was changed by three actions. The War and Navy Departments were combined to form the Department of Defense. To gather information on other nations, the Central Intelligence Agency (CIA) was formed. To give the president a better view of the world, the National Security Council (NSC) was created.

The election of 1948. Truman was chosen by the Democrats as their presidential nominee, but not without bitter arguments. Southern Democrats walked out of the convention to protest Truman's civil rights program, and they formed the States' Rights Democratic Party (Dixiecrats) led by Strom Thurmond. The Henry Wallace faction of the party blamed Truman for the troubles with Russia; they left to form the Progressive Party. The Republicans confidently chose Governor Thomas E. Dewey of New York as their candidate.

Truman blasted "that good-for-nothing 80th Congress" for the nation's troubles in a railroad "whistle stop" campaign. Dewey avoided the tough issues in carefully worded speeches. Even though Truman was far behind in the polls, his efforts paid off. The electoral vote was Truman 303, Dewey 189, and Thurmond 39. The election also put Democrats in control of both Houses of Congress.

TRUMAN AS PRESIDENT (second term). Much of Truman's time during the second term was devoted to foreign problems. Russia was expanding in Europe, and the Communist Chinese were advancing across that nation. West Berlin was like a small island in a Communist sea. In 1948 the city was cut off from the road and railroad bridge that had been its supply line across East Germany. Truman had begun an airlift of supplies to the city, which was an amazing project. A plane carrying supplies arrived at one airport every three minutes, and at another, every two minutes. By 1949, the Russians realized that they had lost and lifted the blockade. The experience had brought the United States and the Germans together, and West Germany was formed in 1949.

A setback for the United States occurred when the Communists drove the Nationalists out of China. The pro-American Nationalists set up their government in Formosa (Taiwan).

The North Atlantic Treaty Organization (NATO) was formed in 1949, and in 1950, General Eisenhower was named its commander. While most American attention was on Europe, war broke out in Korea.

North Korea attacked South Korea, an American ally, in June 1950. Truman acted quickly and sent troops and airplanes to help South Korea. The North Koreans pushed the American and South Korean armies into a small area on the east coast called the Pusan beachhead. General Douglas MacArthur then surprised the North Koreans by an attack on the west coast at Inchon. With more help coming, the North Koreans were pushed back north near China. MacArthur wanted to expand the war, and he violated Truman's orders to limit the war. Finally, Truman fired him. After the war reached a stalemate, peace talks were held, but peace did not come until 1953.

DWIGHT EISENHOWER
(1890–1969, P. 1953–1961)

It was clear in 1952 that the nation was looking for a new kind of leader, one who was experienced in international affairs, had a quiet, unassuming type of personality, who understood military affairs, and was not a Democrat. The leader chosen fit all those qualities and more; he was "Ike" Eisenhower.

Eisenhower was born in Texas but was raised in Abilene, Kansas. His father was a mechanic at a creamery, and the family lived in the poor part of town. When Dwight was a boy, he had blood poisoning in his leg, and the doctor wanted to amputate it. Dwight told his brother, Edgar, to stand at the door and keep the doctor from cutting off his leg. The leg improved in time, and Dwight learned how important willpower was.

Eisenhower entered West Point in 1911. He wanted to play football there, even though he was not a very large young man. He injured his knee while playing and could never play again. He graduated from West Point in 1915. He was then stationed in Texas, where he met Mamie Doud, whom he married in 1916. Most of his early jobs in the army entailed being assistants to others with higher rank. He worked for the assistant secretary of war; he then went to the Philippines as an assistant to General Douglas MacArthur. In 1940, he was named chief of staff of the Third Division. Army men found him likeable, dependable, and able, but they paid him little notice. Then in 1941, General George Marshall saw him as a potential leader and picked him to be his assistant.

By 1942, Eisenhower was the commanding general of the European Theater of Operation in World War II. He was given the job of leading the invasion of North Africa, then Sicily, and Italy. Most important of all, he was named the Supreme Commander of Allied Forces and was in charge of the invasion of Normandy on D-Day. He led his men to victory over Germany. After the war, Eisenhower was named army chief of staff and was in charge of cutting the size of the army.

Eisenhower wrote a book, *Crusade in Europe,* which was published in 1948, and he then served as president of Columbia University for two years. In 1950, he was picked to lead NATO by President Truman. With the war in Korea going badly, both parties wanted Eisenhower as their presidential nominee in the 1952 election. Eisenhower decided he was a Republican.

The election of 1952. The Democrats chose Governor Adlai Stevenson of Illinois as their candidate. He was a very thoughtful, competent man, but he often spoke above the heads of his audience. The two leading Republican candidates were Eisenhower and Senator Robert Taft from Ohio. The more conservative Republicans preferred Taft, but they were overrun by the more liberal Republicans who felt Eisenhower could give the party a great victory in November. The Republican mottoes were: "It's time for a change" and "I like Ike." Eisenhower carried all but nine states, and he won the election 442–89 in electoral votes. For the first time since 1933, a Republican was living in the White House.

EISENHOWER AS PRESIDENT (first term). Eisenhower appointed business leaders to most jobs in his administration. Each was responsible for running his or her department, and was required to send reports to him on what was happening. Whenever anything went wrong, it was the cabinet member, not Eisenhower, whom the public blamed. The key people around the president were John Foster Dulles, secretary of state; Charles Wilson, secretary of defense; and Sherman Adams, his chief of staff. Many problems arose during his first term in office.

The most pressing problem was ending the war in Korea. Eisenhower fulfilled a campaign promise by going to Korea and meeting officers and enlisted men there. The peace talks came to an end after months of arguing. The new line between North and South Korea was very close to where it was when the war started, wavering along or near the 38th parallel.

At home, Senator Joe McCarthy conducted hearings into charges that Communists had sneaked into high positions. People were brought before his committee, and many were accused of being Communists; because of that, many in government, the movie industry, and even Congress were ruined. Eisenhower said he didn't want to get into the gutter with McCarthy. However, after McCarthy accused the army of hiding Communists, a new set of hearings attacked McCarthy himself. He was censured (officially criticized) by the Senate in 1954; he died in 1957.

One of Eisenhower's first appointees was Earl Warren as chief justice of the Supreme Court. In 1954, the Supreme Court handed down the *Brown v. Topeka Board of Education* decision, which said segregation in education violated the 14th Amendment of the Constitution. Some states began allowing black and white students to attend school together, but others refused, which led to trouble in southern schools for years to come.

Another way African-Americans were segregated was on buses. In 1956, Rosa Parks, a black woman, was tired after a day at work and refused to give up her seat to a white man on a bus in Montgomery, Alabama. She was arrested, and blacks refused to ride city buses until they were treated more fairly. The leader of the bus boycott was Dr. Martin Luther King, Jr. In 1956, the Supreme Court ruled that segregation was banned from buses as well.

Other significant issues were addressed. Taxes were cut, more people were made eligible for Social Security, student loans were given to college students, and the building of interstate highways began.

Two serious international problems occurred simultaneously. Egypt decided to take over the Suez Canal, which was owned by British and French investors. The United States was disturbed when paratroops were sent to the Canal by the British and French governments. At the same time, the Russians sent troops into Hungary to put down a revolt against the unpopular Communist government.

Eisenhower's health also became a great concern. He suffered a major heart attack in 1956 but was recovering by the time of the election. In 1956, he easily defeated Adlai Stevenson again.

EISENHOWER AS PRESIDENT (second term). The president faced a number of serious issues during his second term, some at home and some from troubles around the world.

The most serious problem at home was ending segregation of schools in some southern states. Eisenhower did not approve of segregating students, but he thought a gradual approach was best; rushing people into doing something they opposed only brought more friction. On the other hand, he knew the Constitution had to be enforced.

In 1957, nine black students were to be admitted to Little Rock, Arkansas's, Central High School. Riots broke out, and the governor called up the National Guard to keep the black students from attending. After the U.S. District Court ordered the Guard removed, there was little protection for the black students when they came back to school. Riots broke out; Eisenhower federalized 10,000 Arkansas National Guardsmen and then sent in 1,000 paratroopers to keep order.

Progress was very slow, and stubborn opposition caused trouble in many places in the South. When Eisenhower left office, there were still no African-Americans attending school with whites in four states, and less than two percent attended with whites in seven others.

Foreign affairs. The most dangerous situation for all Americans was the Cold War. The threat of a war using atomic and hydrogen weapons terrified some people so much they built bomb shelters behind their homes and stocked them with food and water.

In 1957, the Russians launched the world's first man-made satellite, *Sputnik I*. The United States was stunned. The following year, NASA was formed to begin a strong U.S. space program, and the federal government put money into school science programs.

The Russians felt they had the upper hand now, and they told the West it must give up Berlin in six months or the Russians would turn it over to the East Germans. The NATO members joined together and made it clear they were not going to turn over Berlin. The Russian leader, Nikita Khruschev, realized they meant business and started a public relations effort to show that Russia was a peaceful nation. Khruschev came to the United States and other western nations as well to show his good intentions.

A summit meeting of world leaders was scheduled for Paris in 1960. Just before the summit took place, an American U-2 spy plane was shot down 1,200 miles inside Russian territory. Eisenhower said he knew about the flight, and Khruschev broke up the summit.

A new problem was developing closer to home. The Communist Fidel Castro took over in Cuba, and he let the United States know he was going to take over U.S.-owned businesses in Cuba. Eisenhower allowed Cuban refugees to be trained to overthrow Castro.

Eisenhower remained popular to the end of his terms in office, and the United States remained strong and prosperous.

Name: _____ Date: _____

Points to Ponder (Truman, Eisenhower)

1. Why did people think Truman was not prepared to be president?

   _____

   _____

   _____

   _____

2. Why was the Truman Committee formed?

   _____

   _____

   _____

   _____

3. Why did prices go up so quickly in 1946?

   _____

   _____

   _____

   _____

4. What was the purpose of the Marshall Plan?

   _____

   _____

   _____

   _____

5. How had Eisenhower become famous?

   _____

   _____

   _____

   _____

Points to Ponder (Truman, Eisenhower)

6. What changes did the Korean War make in the boundary between North and South Korea?

    _____

    _____

    _____

    _____

7. What was the importance of the *Brown v. Topeka Board of Education* decision?

    _____

    _____

    _____

    _____

    _____

8. What caused the breakup of the summit conference in Paris in 1960?

    _____

    _____

    _____

★ ★ ★   Explore History   ★ ★ ★

1. Discuss the outcome of the election of 1948. How did the published results differ from the true outcome? Why was Truman's victory in 1948 so surprising? Stage a class debate about the influence and power of the media in today's world. Does the media sometimes go too far in its reporting of events?

2. Research the life and career of one of the following: General Douglas MacArthur, Winston Churchill, or Joseph Stalin. Write a short biography or make a time line about the life of one of these famous men, and include a picture of him.

3. Give an eyewitness account as if you were a member of the National Guard troops ordered by the governor of Arkansas to keep African-American students out of Little Rock Central High School. How did you feel about it?

4. Some Americans built bomb shelters during the 1950s. Write a mini-report. Discuss why they built them and what types of supplies they may have stored there. Do you know anyone who built a bomb shelter?

JOHN F. KENNEDY
(1917–1963, P. 1961–1963)

On a cold January day in 1961, millions watched on television as John F. Kennedy, the youngest man ever to be elected president, took his oath of office. In his inaugural address, he challenged the nation and world: "And so, my fellow Americans, ask not what your country can do for you—ask what you can do for your country. My fellow citizens of the world: ask not what America can do for you, but what together we can do for the freedom of man."

The tensions and struggles of that time have been forgotten by those who remember the glitter of youth during those years. The Kennedy years have often been called "Camelot," when the young new king and his beautiful wife presided over the Round Table, and brave knights went out to slay dragons. There were certainly battles fought and much drama, but good did not always win.

John Fitzgerald Kennedy was born on May 29, 1917, in Brookline, Massachusetts, to a life in politics. On his mother's side, his grandfather had been mayor of Boston, in the U.S. House, and had been defeated in a Senate race by Henry Cabot Lodge. His father, Joseph, was very active in politics as well as business, and he had been appointed to head the Securities and Exchange Commission by President Roosevelt; Joseph Kennedy was later named ambassador to Great Britain. All the Kennedy sons were groomed to become successful in politics. Their names were Joe Jr., John, Robert, and Edward (Ted).

John Kennedy graduated from Harvard in 1940. While his record was not spectacular, his senior thesis, *Why England Slept,* was published. The thesis indicated his belief that weakness produces a dangerous foreign policy.

During World War II, Joe, Jr. was killed in a bombing run over Germany. John had volunteered for the navy and was given command of PT-109, a patrol torpedo boat. It was rammed by a Japanese destroyer. Even though he was badly injured, John towed a crew member five hours to an island, using a strap he held in his mouth. The crew was rescued four days later, and after his recovery in the hospital, Kennedy was discharged with a Navy and Marine Corps Medal.

In 1946, Kennedy ran for the U.S. House from a Boston district and easily won. In 1952, he challenged Henry Cabot Lodge, Jr., for his Senate seat and won by a small margin. He never fit into the Senate mold, but his sights were set on a higher office. In 1956, he tried for the vice presidential nomination but was defeated. However, his effort helped his name to become well known across the nation. While he was recovering from a spinal operation in 1956, he wrote *Profiles in Courage,* which won the Pulitzer Prize.

The election of 1960. In 1960, Kennedy was able to overcome other challengers for the Democratic nomination: Hubert Humphrey and Lyndon Johnson. For vice president, he chose Lyndon Johnson, Senate majority leader from Texas. His Republican opponent was Vice President Richard Nixon. Although Nixon did not personally use the religion issue, many Protestants feared a Catholic would follow orders from the Pope. Kennedy said his duty was to the nation, not to the church.

During the campaign, the first televised debate between the candidates took place, and Kennedy seemed more impressive than Nixon to many people. When the votes were counted, Kennedy had barely won 303–219 in electoral votes. A shift of 23,000 votes in three key states would have elected Nixon instead of Kennedy.

KENNEDY AS PRESIDENT. Kennedy aroused enthusiasm for public service among many young people. His emphasis was on getting things done, and those around him shared his enthusiasm. Among these "New Frontiersmen" as they were called were Robert MacNamara (secretary of defense), Douglas Dillon (a Republican and secretary of the treasury), Dean Rusk (secretary of state), and Kennedy's brother, Robert (attorney general). The public was enchanted with Kennedy's family, and they took countless pictures of his wife, Jacqueline, and their children, Caroline and John, Jr. The Kennedys were pictured at home wearing sweatshirts and playing touch football, as well as in formal clothes attending a concert. Articles about anyone in the Kennedy clan were often published in the United States as well as around the world.

Kennedy won many over with his big smile and clever wit. When a young person asked him how he had become a hero, he said: "It was involuntary; they sank my boat." When some protested about Robert Kennedy being named attorney general without ever having practiced law, Kennedy answered: "I can't see that it's wrong to give him a little legal experience before he goes out to practice law."

Civil rights. The most troubling domestic issue of the time was civil rights. The most prominent civil rights leader was Dr. Martin Luther King, Jr. His approach was peaceful, but firm. If any violence occurred during a demonstration, it would be by the opponent; therefore his actions would turn the nation against himself. The NAACP, the oldest civil rights group, was very effective in courts, winning cases against discrimination. A new group, the Congress of Racial Equality (CORE) used sit-ins and other means to break segregation in bus transportation and at lunch counters.

At first, Kennedy was reluctant to tangle with the southern Democrats in Congress, but where he could act, he did. He increased the numbers of African-Americans in better government jobs: 36 percent in the middle-grade jobs and 88 percent in the top-grade jobs. When CORE "freedom riders" were attacked by mobs at bus depots, 600 deputy U.S. marshals were sent to restore order. The Interstate Commerce Commission ordered segregation ended in terminals.

When the governor of Mississippi refused to admit James Meredith, a well-qualified Air Force veteran, to the University of Mississippi, Robert Kennedy obtained a court order forbidding the governor to interfere. The governor ignored the order. When Meredith arrived on the campus with federal marshals, they were attacked by a mob. President Kennedy federalized the National Guard and order was restored; but by that time, two had been killed and hundreds were injured. In Birmingham, civil rights workers led by Dr. King tangled with crowds at stores and restaurants that refused to serve African-Americans. Police Commissioner "Bull" Connor used clubs, police dogs, and fire hoses to stop street demonstrations.

Kennedy's patience was running out when Governor George Wallace personally blocked blacks from entering the University of Alabama. Kennedy federalized the Alabama National Guard and forced Wallace to back down. Kennedy asked Congress for stronger civil rights laws. Civil rights leaders organized the March on Washington, which brought 250,000 to a dramatic rally at the Lincoln Memorial.

Foreign policy. Cuba gave Kennedy his greatest embarrassment as well as his greatest victory in a test of wills with Fidel Castro and Nikita Khruschev during the Bay of Pigs invasion and the Cuban Missile Crisis. When Kennedy learned that Cuban refugees had been trained for an invasion of Cuba, he was assured by the CIA that they were ready. He gave the green light for the invasion but told them the United States would provide no aid if the attack faltered. They landed April 17, 1961, and 1,000 were captured. The invasion was a complete failure.

Khruschev, Russia's leader, must have decided that the United States was in weak hands, and he again threatened to turn West Berlin over to East Germany. Kennedy did not budge on this issue, and asked Congress for the power to call up reserves. He then increased the number of draftees and told the United States: "We seek peace, but we shall not surrender." Instead of merely threatening, Russia built a wall around West Berlin. Kennedy sent 1,500 more troops into Berlin. The Russians backed off, and the crisis passed.

The Cold War reached a climax when in 1962, the Russians planned to put nuclear weapons on missiles based in Cuba. The missiles had a range of up to 2,000 miles, which could easily reach many of the major cities in the United States. The United States put a blockade around Cuba and threatened to search any ship within a zone around the island. The tension grew as Russian ships carrying missiles came close to the blockade, but at the last minute they were ordered to return home. To help prevent future crises, the "hot line" was installed that summer between the White House and the Kremlin.

The war in Vietnam continued despite the line that had been drawn in 1954. The pro-American South Vietnamese government was unpopular with the public there. To win the war, the United States was beginning to play a more important role. Kennedy sent well-trained troops, the Green Berets, to show the South Vietnamese army how to fight more effectively.

On November 22, 1963, while in a motorcade in Dallas, Texas, the president was shot by a gunman from the window of a six-story building. Kennedy was rushed to the hospital, and he died minutes later. His body was flown to Washington as a stunned nation watched. The gunman, Lee Harvey Oswald, was captured, but on November 24 he was shot and killed by a nightclub operator Jack Ruby. Kennedy is buried in Arlington National Cemetery.

LYNDON B. JOHNSON
(1908–1973, P. 1963–1969)

The death of President Kennedy brought great sadness to the nation, and again a vice president was taking the oath of office. Johnson was unusually well prepared for the assignment, and for a time his popularity was very high. He knew how to get things done, and some bills that had gone nowhere in the Kennedy years became laws. Then came a changing mood in the nation, and Johnson was hated and booed out of office.

Lyndon grew up in a very political family, living in the sandhills of southwest Texas. His family was not as poor as some, but they knew that only hard work would produce the money they needed. As a boy, he did various odd jobs, from picking cotton and shining shoes to waiting tables and washing dishes. He graduated from Southwest Texas State Teachers College in 1930 and taught for a while. He worked hard for the "Kleberg for Congress" campaign; when Kleberg won, he took Johnson to Washington as his secretary. In 1934, Johnson married Claudia (nicknamed Lady Bird) Taylor, whose father was a wealthy oil man. The next year he went back to Texas to lead the National Youth Administration (NYA), where he found jobs for many of the state's college students.

In 1937, Johnson was elected to the U.S. House, where he was a good "New Dealer" and became popular with Roosevelt. He was soon known as a man who got things done for his district and his state. In 1941, Johnson was defeated in a close special election to fill a vacant Senate seat. That same year, he was given special leave by the House to go into active service in the Navy Reserve and was commissioned as lieutenant commander. In 1942, he received the Silver Star for gallantry under fire. After FDR ordered all members of Congress serving in the armed forces to return home, his active career in the navy ended, but he continued in the Naval Reserves.

In 1948, Johnson was elected senator from Texas and was named to the Armed Services Committee. He was often critical of Truman's conduct during the Korean War. Unlike some Democrats, he cooperated with Eisenhower's Republican administration. He said: "Any jackass can kick down a barn. It takes a good carpenter to build a barn. We aim to build."

In 1953, he was elected Senate minority leader, and after the 1954 election, he became majority leader. True to his word, he played a constructive part in helping Eisenhower get bills through Congress. In 1957, he was active in getting the civil rights bill passed that Eisenhower had asked for. He favored a larger Air Force after the Russians launched *Sputnik I.* Then he chaired the Senate committee that created NASA.

When it appeared that Kennedy might win the party nomination in 1960, Johnson received support from some southern and western delegations that wanted to block Kennedy. The effort failed, but in a surprising move, Kennedy chose Johnson for vice president.

Vice President Johnson was much busier than most men in his office had been in the past. He made good-will trips, sat in on cabinet meetings, and discussed legislation with Congressmen. Few vice presidents had ever been as well informed as Johnson was when tragedy elevated them to the presidential office.

JOHNSON AS PRESIDENT (first term). Johnson was determined to be a president who got things accomplished. Johnson knew he had less than a year to convince the voters he was worthy of their votes, so he pressured his former colleagues in the House and Senate to pass bills quickly. Important legislation, long-buried in committee, was suddenly brought to a vote.

The Civil Rights Act of 1964 overcame strong opposition in the Senate with the help of Republican Senator Everett Dirksen. The act made it illegal to bar anyone from a hotel, restaurant, barbershop, or place of amusement on the basis of their race. It cut off federal programs to any community that allowed discrimination.

Taxes were reduced by over $11 billion. Congress voted money to combat poverty. Job training programs were increased, and more money was put into federal education programs.

The election of 1964. While some disagreement is common, in 1964, the presidential candidates represented opposite views on almost every major topic. In the Republican primaries, the more liberal members were split between several candidates, while the conservatives were united behind Barry Goldwater, a senator from Arizona. He had voted against the civil rights law, wanted to make Social Security voluntary, and was critical of the TVA and many other government programs. It was easy for his opponents to take his statements out of context and use them against him.

When votes were counted in November, Johnson won by 27 million popular votes and by 486–52 in electoral votes. Democrats also gained more seats in Congress, with 295 to 140 in the House and 68 to 32 in the Senate. The Republicans had carried only six states, five of those in the South. While it was not recognized at the time, this election was the beginning of a strong Republican presence in the South.

JOHNSON AS PRESIDENT (second term). Johnson's second term began with the passage of Medicare, a program to help the elderly pay for medical expenses. There were new, large grants for education, from elementary schools to aid for colleges. A program to help Appalachia was approved. The amount being used to fight poverty was doubled. The Voting Rights Act was passed in 1965 to protect the African-American's right to register and vote. The Twenty-fourth Amendment was ratified, making the poll tax unconstitutional.

In 1966, the record of successes began to develop a backlash. The public was beginning to wonder if bigger programs and more government involvement had gone too far. In the election of 1966, the Democrats lost 47 seats in the House and three in the Senate.

Two major problems divided Americans for many years to come.

Race. Johnson's efforts to solve the unfairness in the way African-Americans were treated had centered on the south. However, many blacks lived in northern cities where different problems existed. Young blacks in the north were more militant, and they began forming groups that spoke in terms of revolution and violence. One young leader said that "violence is as American as cherry pie." Riots broke out in northern cities. The worst riot was in the Watts section of Los Angeles, which left 34 dead, hundreds injured, and many buildings burned.

The Kerner Commission studied the racial tension, and said in its 1968 report: "Our nation is moving toward two societies, one black, one white—separate but unequal."

Vietnam. The war in Vietnam had been going on since 1947. At first, the rebels wanted to drive the French out, and they succeeded in 1954. Vietnam was divided that year between the Communists in North Vietnam led by Ho Chi Minh and the anti-Communist government in

South Vietnam, with its capital in Saigon. Kennedy had previously sent a few thousand troops to help train the South Vietnamese army, but their efforts had failed. Now a group of anti-American Communist rebels in the south, who were called the Viet Cong, were fighting against the South Vietnamese army and the Americans. Supplies from the Communists in the north were being sent through neighboring Cambodia and Laos to help the Viet Cong.

Johnson waited until after the 1964 election to send larger numbers of troops to Vietnam, with the purpose of showing so much force that North Vietnam would make peace. In November 1965, there were 165,000 U.S. troops in Vietnam; and more were being sent. By 1968, the number had reached 543,000. Despite predictions that victory was around the corner, victory seemed no nearer than before.

Protests by college students soon to be drafted became a common occurrence. The famous boxer Muhammad Ali refused to be inducted into the Army saying: "I ain't got no quarrel with them Viet Cong." That inspired others to burn their draft cards or flee to Canada to avoid the draft. Johnson's popularity was dropping, both in Congress and on the streets. In 1968, he announced he would not run for another term.

In April, Dr. King was assassinated in Memphis, and after winning the California presidential primary that summer, Robert Kennedy was assassinated. Johnson's vice president, Hubert Humphrey, was defeated in 1968, and the former vice president, Richard Nixon, was elected.

Name: _____ Date: _____

Points to Ponder (Kennedy, L. Johnson)

1. How did Kennedy become a naval hero?

_____

_____

_____

_____

_____

2. What did Kennedy do when "freedom riders" were attacked at bus stations?

_____

_____

_____

_____

3. What happened at the Bay of Pigs, and what did Khruschev do because of it?

_____

_____

_____

_____

_____

4. Why was the Cuban Missile Crisis so tense? What prevented a major war from occurring?

_____

_____

_____

_____

_____

5. Why were the Green Berets sent to Vietnam?

_____

_____

_____

_____

Name: _____ Date: _____

Points to Ponder (Kennedy, L. Johnson)

6. What experience did Johnson have that helped him get his programs through Congress from 1964 through 1966?

    _____

    _____

    _____

7. Why was the Civil Rights Act of 1964 so important?

    _____

    _____

    _____

8. What was voter reaction to Goldwater and other Republican candidates in 1964?

    _____

    _____

9. How did young, urban African-Americans react to Johnson?

    _____

    _____

10. What was Johnson's goal in the Vietnam War? How did the public react to increased U.S. involvement in the war?

    _____

    _____

    _____

☆ ☆ ☆ **Explore History** ☆ ☆ ☆

1. Part of Kennedy's inaugural address, "and so, my fellow Americans..." is often quoted. List other famous quotations by former presidents.

2. Research NASA and the Apollo Space Program. Write a report, build a model, or make a drawing of an Apollo spacecraft.

3. Find or draw a picture of a patrol torpedo boat such as Kennedy's PT-109.

4. Conduct an interview or a debate regarding civil rights with Martin Luther King, Jr.; J. Edgar Hoover; or Malcolm X.

RICHARD NIXON
(1913–1994, P. 1969–1974)

President Nixon had survived many battles in his political life, but it became clear in the summer of 1974 he would not overcome the opposition this time, and he resigned as president. For all his knowledge of the art of politics, he had blundered in a colossal way in the campaign of 1972. It cost him his job and reputation.

Nixon was born in Yorba Linda, California, in 1913, into a poor but hardworking family. Richard graduated from Whittier College as student body president in 1934, and he received a scholarship to Duke University School of Law, from which he graduated near the top of his class in 1937. After five years of practicing law, he joined the navy in 1942 and was sent to the Pacific as an officer. He was discharged in 1946.

He ran for Congress in 1946 as a Republican and was named to the House Un-American Activities Committee (HUAC). There, he became famous for his attacks on Alger Hiss, a former State Department official accused of having been a Communist. In 1950, Nixon won a hard-fought campaign for the U.S. Senate, in which he accused his opponent of being a Communist stooge. His reputation as a leader of conservative Republicans made him a possible running mate for Eisenhower, a middle-of-the-road Republican.

After he was chosen, Nixon was accused of having $18,000 of his living expenses as a senator paid for by a group of wealthy businessmen. As a result, he appeared on television with his wife, his daughters, and his dog "Checkers." He then stated that the only gift he had received was the dog, which had been given to his daughters. Thousands of letters were received from all over the country in support of keeping Nixon on the ticket.

As vice president, he was sent as Eisenhower's representative into some tough situations. On one trip he was sent to Latin America, and his motorcade was surrounded by angry protesters who rocked his limousine back and forth.

In 1960, Nixon ran for president against John Kennedy and lost by a small margin. Two years later, he ran for governor in California and lost again. At that point, he was ready to quit politics, and he told the press, whom he blamed for his defeat, "Now you won't have Nixon to kick around anymore." His vacation from politics did not last long, however, and in 1964, he was one of the few Republicans campaigning hard for Goldwater. His party loyalty was rewarded with the party nomination for president in 1968.

The campaign of 1968. Nixon's opponents in the 1968 Republican race were Nelson Rockefeller from New York and California's governor, Ronald Reagan, but Nixon was nominated on the first ballot. For vice president, he chose Maryland's governor, Spiro Agnew. Nixon's Democratic opponent was Vice President Hubert Humphrey, who had a difficult situation, getting support from Johnson Democrats without losing the newly formed anti-Vietnam War demonstrators. A third candidate, George Wallace, created a new ticket, the American Independence Party, which was against integration of schools and in favor of law and order. Wallace was more likely to take votes from Nixon than Humphrey. By the end of the campaign, Humphrey was gaining on Nixon, but he lost in a close contest. In electoral votes, Nixon won by 301–191 over Humphrey; Wallace came in third with a respectable 46 electoral votes. In popular vote, Nixon won by only a half-million votes over Humphrey.

NIXON AS PRESIDENT (first term). Nixon had been elected president, but the Democrats controlled Congress. He could not always control spending, but he found a way around that problem. Nixon simply refused to spend all the money that had been budgeted for some programs; he rarely called cabinet meetings and ignored many of his "official" family. Instead, he turned to other advisors, some of whom became especially important. Henry Kissinger, a Harvard professor, became his National Security Advisor; H.R. Haldeman, an advertising executive, became his chief of staff; John Mitchell, another close friend, was named attorney general.

Inflation became a more serious issue during Nixon's first term. Reasons for inflation were the cost of fighting the Vietnam War, rising food prices, and the cost of gasoline. OPEC, a group of oil producing countries, began cutting back on production and prices increased slowly at first, then jumped quickly in 1973.

Supreme Court appointments are important choices for a president. Nixon wanted conservatives on the Court who were likely to support his positions on limiting defendants' rights and other issues. Warren Burger, a moderate, was chosen as chief justice. Then two men he chose for associate justice vacancies were rejected by the Senate. Nixon then chose three able men to fill vacancies. Once chosen, however, a Supreme Court justice makes decisions that sometimes surprise, and even oppose, the president who chose them.

Foreign policy. Nixon had always been strongly anti-Communist, but as president, he realized that circumstances change, and the United States needed to use those changes to its advantage. He and his foreign affairs advisor, Dr. Henry Kissinger, began to change United States policies that had been held since the beginning of the Cold War.

Anti-war protests were common in 1969 and 1970; many colleges had closed because of them. Nixon began pulling U.S. troops out of South Vietnam and relying on bombing attacks on the North to end the war. U.S. troop numbers dropped from 543,000 to 39,000 in 1972.

The Soviet Union and China were clearly unfriendly with each other, and Nixon saw an opportunity to improve relations with China. In 1972, he made a trip to China that went well. A few months later, he visited Moscow, and agreements were made to limit arms and increase trade.

The election of 1972. Nixon was going strong by 1972, and Republicans were united behind him. The Democrats, on the other hand, were divided into warring camps. Older Democrats preferred Ted Kennedy, Edmund Muskie, or Hubert Humphrey. Young Democrats rallied behind Senator George McGovern, who was anti-Vietnam War and wanted to pull all U.S. troops out. McGovern was chosen as the party candidate, but he had angered many party members in the process.

Nothing went right for McGovern. Because other speakers droned on, he did not give his acceptance speech until 3:00 A.M. His running mate, Senator Thomas Eagleton, was dropped because he had once had electric shock treatments for depression. After burglars were caught inside Democratic headquarters at the Watergate complex, McGovern charged that it was a Republican plot, but most Americans assumed he was just grasping at straws. The McGovern campaign was starved for money, while big donations flooded into Nixon headquarters.

NIXON AS PRESIDENT (second term). The election was a clear victory for Nixon, who received over 60 percent of the popular vote; McGovern won only in Massachusetts and the District of Columbia. As often happens in politics, the glory of the moment was short, and dark days lay ahead. In 1973, Vice President Agnew was forced to resign because of criminal charges brought against him. Nixon chose Gerald Ford as his new vice president. Then Watergate and its cover-up became the focus of attention.

Vietnam. To help South Vietnam, which was losing badly to the North, Nixon began bombing attacks on Viet Cong supply lines through Laos and Cambodia. Campus demonstrations began again, and at Kent State University in Ohio, National Guardsmen killed four students.

Watergate. For the 1972 campaign, Nixon assembled a group of zealous supporters willing to do anything to win. Heading the Committee to Re-Elect the President (dubbed CREEP) was former Attorney General Mitchell. A group was sent to Democratic headquarters to plant listening devices. They were caught but refused to talk. The judge sentenced them to 20 years in prison. One of those convicted told the judge they had been sent by CREEP. Others began to talk to save themselves. Another said conversations had been held in the president's office to cover up CREEP's part in the affair. This was denied by Mitchell and Nixon, but then it was learned there was a taping machine in the office.

The Supreme Court in a 9–0 decision ordered Nixon to turn over some of the tapes to a special prosecutor. When the contents were revealed, impeachment proceedings were begun by the House. The House Judiciary Committee voted to impeach the president, and Nixon resigned rather than face a Senate trial. Trials for Watergate defendants continued for months, and many of those involved served prison time. Nixon was pardoned by President Ford.

Nixon lived long enough after leaving office to improve his reputation, and he gave helpful advice to other presidents on foreign affairs. Watergate remains a topic for speculation, and people wonder how someone as intelligent as Nixon could have permitted such a blunder.

GERALD FORD
(1913–2006, P. 1974–1977)

No fortuneteller could have predicted the circumstances that made it possible for Gerald Ford to become president in 1972. He had not been chosen for president or vice president and had been very content to serve his Michigan district and as minority leader in the House. But these were unusual times, and after only a few months as vice president, he took the oath of office as president. As his wife put it, he was an "accidental vice president, and an accidental president, and in both jobs he replaced disgraced leaders."

Ford's original name was Leslie King, and he was born in Omaha, Nebraska, in 1913. After his parents divorced, his mother moved to Grand Rapids, Michigan, where he was adopted by his stepfather and renamed Gerald R. Ford. While there, he was captain of his high school football team. He received a football scholarship to the University of Michigan where he was an outstanding center on the team for three years. The 1932 and 1933 teams went undefeated, and he was chosen as the most valuable player in 1934. Yale University chose him as an assistant coach, which made it possible for him to attend Yale Law School. He graduated in the top third of his class in 1941. Ford then returned to Grand Rapids to practice law.

In 1942, he joined the navy and was an officer on an aircraft carrier in the South Pacific. After his discharge in 1946, he returned to Grand Rapids and his law practice. Two years later, he married Elizabeth (Betty) Bloomer. He was elected to the House in 1948, and he served for 13 terms. In the House, he was a conservative who, in his own words, was moderate on domestic policy, a conservative on financial issues, and was in favor of the United States playing an important role in world affairs.

In 1973, Vice President Agnew was forced to resign, and acting under the Twenty-fifth Amendment, President Nixon chose Ford as the new vice president. He was approved by both Houses of Congress. The importance of that change in job was becoming more clear. President Nixon was fighting charges of covering up the Watergate break-in, and after the Supreme Court ordered Nixon to turn over the White House tapes, the House Judiciary Committee voted to impeach the president. He resigned before the Senate trial began. On August 9, 1974, Ford took the presidential oath of office.

FORD AS PRESIDENT. The public had complained for years that presidents acted like kings with large staffs to serve them. Ford quickly showed that he was different. When his dog made a mess, he cleaned it up himself. Ford liked to fix his own breakfast in the morning. His old friends in Congress talked about how friendly he was, and despite some bitter arguments, a long-time opponent said Ford had no enemies.

In September 1974, Ford granted a pardon to President Nixon, explaining that it was to begin the national healing process after Watergate and to save Nixon and his family from further suffering. A week later, he granted an amnesty (forgiveness) for many of those who had evaded the draft or deserted from the armed forces during the Vietnam War. The Nixon pardon was very unpopular, and Ford thought it may have cost him the election of 1976.

For vice president, Ford chose Nelson Rockefeller, who had served in the federal government and had been governor of New York for 15 years. Rockefeller was approved by Congress in December 1974.

Domestic policies. The main problems Ford faced were high unemployment and inflation. Before acting on them, he held an economic conference to look for the best way to solve these problems. He tried to control inflation by cutting some government programs, and when Congress tried to put money back into cut budgets, he vetoed the bills. During his time in office, inflation dropped from 11.2 percent to 5.3 percent. In 1975, he proposed tax cuts, but most of his efforts to improve the economy failed to convince Congress.

Foreign affairs. Ford kept Henry Kissinger as his secretary of state, and worked to improve relations with the Soviet Union. In 1975, he traveled to Helsinki, Finland, where he signed an agreement with the Russians promising to honor European borders.

The situation in Vietnam continued to worsen, and Ford did not want to be the president who lost the war. In 1975, the United States pumped more aid into South Vietnam and Cambodia, but by March the governments of both countries were in danger of total collapse. An airlift of children out of Vietnam began early in April. In mid-April, Cambodia surrendered to Communist forces. On April 24, a major airlift of Vietnamese to Guam began. By April 27, Saigon was being shelled, and the president ordered a helicopter evacuation to begin for those Americans still in Vietnam. The last helicopters left April 29 as Communist forces entered the city. South Vietnam surrendered the next day.

The war had cost the United States nearly 58,000 men and $150 billion. It had been the nation's longest and least popular war.

The election of 1976. To get the party nomination, Ford had to fight off those conservatives who liked Governor Ronald Reagan of California more. The contest was close from the very beginning, but at the convention Ford won the nomination by only 117 votes. Ford chose Senator Bob Dole of Kansas as his running mate. Like Reagan, the Democratic candidate, former Governor Jimmy Carter of Georgia, appealed to many as an outsider who was not part of the Washington crowd.

Carter got off to an early lead in the polls, but Ford moved up in the latter days of the campaign. In the end, Ford lost the popular vote by 1.7 million and the electoral vote by 240 to 297. The Democrats had large majorities in both houses of Congress.

After the Fords left public life, Mrs. Ford was treated for alcoholism. She later started the Betty Ford Center in 1982, which has treated many people for addictions ever since.

Name: _____ Date: _____

Points to Ponder (Nixon, Ford)

1. How did Nixon become well known?

   _____

   _____

   _____

2. Why did Nixon make the "Checkers" speech?

   _____

   _____

   _____

3. Why did it appear that his political career was over in 1962?

   _____

   _____

   _____

4. Why did oil prices go up in 1973? Do you think it helped or hurt Nixon?

   _____

   _____

   _____

5. How did Gerald Ford become vice president?

   _____

   _____

   _____

6. What was the importance of the taping machine in Nixon's office?

   _____

   _____

   _____

Name: _____   Date: _____

Points to Ponder (Nixon, Ford)

7. What ruined any chance Nixon had of avoiding impeachment?

_____

_____

_____

_____

8. How did Gerald Ford become president?

_____

_____

_____

_____

9. What did Ford give as the reason he pardoned Nixon? What was the public's reaction?

_____

_____

_____

_____

10. What happened in Cambodia and South Vietnam in 1975?

_____

_____

_____

_____

⭐ ⭐ ⭐   **Explore History**   ⭐ ⭐ ⭐

1. How many different presidents were involved in sending troops to Vietnam? Make a time line.

2. Make a chart or poster listing which presidents were lawyers.

3. Write a short biography about Henry Kissinger.

4. Interview someone who was a "witness" to Watergate. Write an article.

JIMMY CARTER
(1924–   , P. 1977–1981)

"Hello, I'm Jimmy Carter, and I'm running for president." With those words spoken in a soft Georgian accent, Carter shook hands with the people of New Hampshire in one of the most unusual election victories in history.

Carter was born in Plains, Georgia, in 1924, the son of a well-to-do farmer whose black workers lived in small cottages nearby. His father strongly favored segregation, but his mother was kind and open with the workers. Jimmy was more influenced by his mother on that subject, and became a good friend to many African-Americans. The most commented-on trait of young Jimmy Carter was his refusal to quit on anything, whether it was school work or an argument. He set an early goal of graduating from the Naval Academy at Annapolis.

In 1941, Jimmy entered Georgia Southwestern College while waiting for a letter inviting him to attend the Naval Academy. The letter finally arrived, but he would enter the Academy in the summer of 1943 rather than 1942. He switched to Georgia Tech and was accepted into the NROTC unit there to prepare for Annapolis. The Naval Academy was tough for the students, but Carter studied hard. On leave before his third year at the Academy, he fell in love with Rosalynn Smith. Graduating in the top 10 percent of his class, Carter received his commission as an ensign and married Rosalynn.

After serving on surface ships for two years, Carter chose to enter the submarine service. He became an expert on subs, and was proud of his record. He then met Admiral Hyman Rickover, a legend in the Navy for his work on building the submarine service. He asked Carter about his class rank at Annapolis and then asked if he had done his best. Carter admitted he had not. Rickover asked: "Why not?" Rickover became Carter's boss and hero; from Rickover, he learned the importance of detailed planning.

Carter's plans for a Navy career suddenly changed when his father died in 1953 and his mother asked him to take over the family farm. He resigned from the Navy and returned to Plains in 1954. Carter was elected to the Georgia Senate in 1962, failed to win the governor's race in 1966, but won in 1970. His administration was notable for several things. He did not use the race issue; he improved efficiency in government and started new social programs without increasing taxes. In 1972, Carter began exploring the possibility of running for president while speaking around the U.S. as chairman of the Democratic Campaign Committee.

The campaign of 1976. Carter was a unique candidate for president. He started out with little money, and no one had heard of him in the early primary states. He was not apologetic about being a "born-again" Christian, strongly motivated by religion. His campaign was about character, and he wanted government to represent the honest and decent side of Americans. He was the outsider untarnished by scandals.

President Ford fought off a challenge from Ronald Reagan for the Republican nomination, but Carter won a narrow victory in the election.

CARTER AS PRESIDENT. Instead of riding home from his inauguration, Carter and his family walked, waving to people along the way. He preferred the informal approach, and while he dressed like a president should, his staff often wore blue jeans to work. Instead of focusing on one problem, he often proposed many programs at one time, and a reluctant Congress was slow to respond to his requests.

Domestic affairs. Carter had criticized Ford for high inflation and unemployment. Despite Carter's efforts, prices kept going up, reaching 20 percent inflation in 1980. It now took $1 to buy what would have cost 15 cents in 1940.

Part of the reason for higher prices was the cost of energy; Americans were driving bulky, gas-guzzling cars rather than compact and fuel-efficient cars. Oil refineries were cutting back on production, increasing suspicions that the prices were not justified. Another reason for higher prices was the cost of electrical energy, partly caused by the use of fossil fuels. Nuclear power plants had been seen as the way to cut energy costs, but a nuclear accident at Three Mile Island in Pennsylvania caused a near-tragedy. Congress finally approved a program to cut dependence on foreign oil by promoting programs to produce more coal, solar, and wind-produced electricity.

Foreign affairs. The United States faced many issues during the Carter years. Some changes came because of Carter's concern about human rights. He was very critical of nations that abused their own citizens, and he listed South Africa, North Korea, and the Soviet Union, among others, as the worst offenders.

The Panama Canal had been a trouble spot for Ford, and he had been strongly criticized by conservative Republicans when he suggested it should be given to Panama to control. The issue was still being argued when Carter became president. It was only with great effort that a treaty was made to turn the Canal over to Panama by the year 2000.

U.S. relations with China improved, and the two nations began exchanging ambassadors; trade between the United States and China began. However, U.S. relations with the Soviet Union worsened after Russian troops moved into Afghanistan. The United States led an international boycott of the Olympic Games in Moscow.

Carter's greatest success was in bringing Israeli Prime Minister Begin and Egyptian President Sadat to talks at Camp David, which resulted in the peace treaty signed in 1979.

Carter's greatest defeat was in relations with Iran. Anti-American Muslim leaders, led by the Ayatollah Khomeini, had overthrown the Shah (ruler) of Iran. With government approval, students stormed the U.S. embassy in Teheran, captured the Americans there, and held them hostage. U.S. efforts to rescue the hostages failed. Americans rallied behind the hostages and put yellow ribbons around trees. The Iranian hostage crisis became a symbol of Carter's failures, and it led to the election of Ronald Reagan in 1980.

Many people consider Jimmy Carter a much more successful ex-president than he was a president. His peace-keeping and humanitarian efforts since leaving office have led to a favorable opinion of Carter worldwide. In 1982, Jimmy and Rosalynn established The Carter Center in Atlanta, Georgia, to advance human rights and alleviate unnecessary human suffering. In 1994, Carter was sent on peace-keeping missions to Haiti and North Korea by President Bill Clinton. Carter met with Fidel Castro of Cuba in 2002. He has also worked to promote fair elections in South America, Europe, Africa, and the Middle East. In 2002, Carter received the Nobel Peace Prize for his work through the Carter Center "to find peaceful solutions to international conflicts, to advance democracy and human rights, and to promote economic and social development." He was also awarded the Presidential Medal of Freedom in 1999.

RONALD REAGAN
(1911–2004, P. 1981–1989)

Ronald Reagan was the son of a poor family in Illinois. His career included sports broadcasting and acting in movies and television before moving into politics. He was a fine-looking man with great charm, optimism, and ambition, who had climbed the ladder of success. In 1980, he won the election and became president.

Reagan grew up in Dixon, Illinois. His father was an alcoholic and held poor-paying jobs. Ronald sold popcorn at high school games and worked as a lifeguard in the summer to earn the money to attend college. Reagan played football and was in college theatrical productions while attending Eureka College in Illinois; he received his degree in 1932. After graduating, he became a well-known sportscaster in Des Moines, Iowa.

In 1937, Warner Brothers hired Reagan as an actor. He often appeared in "B" movies, but he was known as hard-working, reliable, and prepared. During World War II, he enlisted in the army and made training and morale-boosting films. He held the rank of captain when he was discharged.

After the war, Reagan returned to Hollywood, but his movie career was not successful; in 1951, he made the movie *Bedtime for Bonzo,* in which the star was a chimpanzee. Fortunately, television was growing, and he became the host for *General Electric Theater* and later *Death Valley Days.* His marriage to actress Jane Wyman ended in divorce. His 1952 marriage to actress Nancy Davis helped to change him from a Roosevelt New Deal Democrat into a conservative Republican. Some of the change came from watching lazy civil service employees during the war. He was also concerned about Communist influence in the film industry while he served as president of the Screen Actors Guild.

Small groups of wealthy Republicans suggested that Reagan run for governor of California in 1966. He promised to cut taxes and won by over a million votes. He put a hiring freeze on state jobs but was unable to persuade the legislature to lower taxes. In time, he learned to work with the legislature and to use television as a method of gaining public support. In 1972 and 1976, he tried to win the Republican nomination for president, but the times were not right. So he waited for a more conservative mood to develop in the United States. By 1980, the nation was ready for a change.

The election of 1980. The Democrats were split between those who liked Carter and the liberals who liked Ted Kennedy; the two groups did not come together even at the convention. Reagan also had competition, and two candidates were still working against him until the end: John Anderson and George Bush. Reagan prevailed, and then he chose Bush for vice president. Anderson went on to form a new National Unity Party.

The campaign had the usual number of mistakes by both candidates, but the themes were clear. Carter believed the nation was in a mess and needed his leadership. Reagan believed the problem was Carter. In their debate, Reagan asked the public: "Are you better off than you were four years ago?" "Is America as respected throughout the world as it was?" Nothing that happened afterward helped Carter's cause.

The Reagan victory was even greater than anyone anticipated. He not only had 489 electoral votes to Carter's 49, but he also won by 8.3 million popular votes. Anderson received only seven percent of the popular vote.

REAGAN AS PRESIDENT. Reagan was a far different type of leader than Carter had been. He was cheerful and optimistic. Even when he was rolled into the operating room for a gunshot wound, he asked if the surgeons were all good Republicans.

Reagan's approach to his job was to let each official do his job. Reagan spoke in general outlines, and his officials worked out the details. When problems occurred, the official was the one in trouble with the public and press, not the president. His critics began calling him the "Teflon president" because he rarely got the blame for mistakes.

Economic problems were serious. Inflation and unemployment were high. Reagan's solution was called "supply side economics." He would reduce taxes to encourage business expansion. In 1981, taxes dropped five percent, and in 1982 and 1983, another ten percent. The government cut costs by reducing social programs like welfare benefits, unemployment compensation, and low-cost housing; and grants for college students became student loans. At the same time, he was determined to increase defense spending, which by 1985 had reached $300 billion.

Another change occurred when the federal government started giving states "revenue sharing" money to be spent wherever they thought necessary, with only a few strings attached.

In 1982, the worst recession in many years occurred, and thousands of workers were unemployed, but by the next year, conditions had improved.

Tax money never came close to paying the cost of government, and the budget deficit rose from $74 billion in 1980 to $221 billion in 1986. The national debt was $914 billion in 1980, and $3.1 trillion in 1990.

The election of 1984. The Democratic candidate, former Vice President Walter Mondale, chose as his running mate the first woman to run on a national ticket, Geraldine Ferraro. Mondale was never able to gain much momentum in the campaign, and he lost to Reagan by 525–13 in electoral votes and by nearly 17 million popular votes.

Foreign policy. Reagan saw the Soviet Union as an enemy, an "evil empire." He saw the country as not someone to make friends with, but as an opponent to be destroyed. In 1985, his Reagan Doctrine said we would help any nation that was struggling against Communism. There were many trouble spots around the world, and the United States often became involved in them.

In Afghanistan, a civil war was going on between the Communist-controlled government supported by the Soviet Union and Afghan Muslims who were like those who ruled Iran. The United States sent support to the Afghan rebels.

Libya was ruled by Muammar Qadaffi, who was suspected of using his oil money to help terrorist groups in other countries. The United States found that he was helping terrorists in Germany, and American planes dropped bombs on some Libyan cities.

Iran and Iraq were at war, and the United States helped Iraq by guarding the Persian Gulf. One of the U.S. ships was attacked by an Iraqi plane. In 1988, the United States shot down an Iranian airliner by accident.

Central America. The United States supported an unpopular government in El Salvador that was fighting rebels. In 1983, a new leader was elected and Congress was more than willing to send help. Nicaragua had a government that supported Communism (Sandinistas), and there were rebels who were trying to overthrow it (Contras). Many in Congress felt that the Contras were as bad as the Sandinistas, and they passed laws against military aid to the Contras. A group of White House officials thought of a way around the law; they sold supplies to Iran at a very low price, then in turn, Iran sent aid to the Contras. When this was discovered by the press, it was called "Irangate." No one was sure whether Reagan had known what was happening.

It was in relations with the Soviet Union that Reagan policies showed surprising flexibility. He had been an enemy of the "evil empire," and at first it looked as if he was preparing for a war with them. Defense spending shot up, battleships came out of mothballs, new weapons systems were developed, and Pershing II missiles were set up in West Germany that could reach Russian targets in five minutes. The Russians began building up their military power as well.

At this time a new weapons proposal was pushed by Reagan, called the Strategic Defense Initiative (SDI). This program would put satellites in space, which would be capable of shooting down incoming missiles. Critics said it would not work, that it was terribly expensive, and that it might even encourage a reckless president to attack a nation with nuclear weapons.

In time, Reagan's attitude toward the Soviets softened. Some say it was because Secretary of State George Schultz became more influential with him, or it may have been changes in the Kremlin. From 1982 to 1985, the Soviet Union was led by two elderly premiers; then 54-year-old Mikhail Gorbachev was chosen. Gorbachev began changes that eventally led to democracy.

Gorbachev was eager to develop better relations with the United States. Reagan saw the changes as good for peace, and he attended meetings in Switzerland and Iceland with the Russian leader. Agreements were made to destroy many of the missiles on both sides. While neither side was prepared to call off the Cold War completely, great progress was made.

Reagan returned to private life as a very popular person. After several years of retirement, Reagan developed Alzheimer's disease and remained out of the public eye. He died on June 5, 2004, at his Bel Air, California, home.

Name: _____ Date: _____

Points to Ponder (Carter, Reagan)

1. What lessons did Carter learn from Admiral Rickover?

   _____

   _____

   _____

   _____

2. Why did Carter's success in 1976 surprise many Americans?

   _____

   _____

   _____

3. Why didn't the United States build more nuclear power plants in the Carter years?

   _____

   _____

   _____

4. How did the United States get along with China and Russia while Carter was president?

   _____

   _____

   _____

5. What jobs had Reagan held that taught him how to be "the great communicator," as he was often called?

   _____

   _____

   _____

6. What was the idea behind "supply side economics"?

   _____

   _____

   _____

   _____

Name: _____ Date: _____

Points to Ponder (Carter, Reagan)

7. What happened to the budget and national debt while Reagan was in office?

_____

_____

_____

8. Why did the United States help the Afghan rebels? _____

_____

_____

_____

9. What was "Irangate"? _____

_____

_____

_____

10. What improvements were made in United States-Soviet relations by Reagan and Gorbachev?

_____

_____

_____

☆ ☆ ☆ Explore History ☆ ☆ ☆

1. Make a chart on different types of energy and ways to conserve it.

2. Research the boycotted Moscow Olympic Games of 1980: some athletes lost their chance to compete for an Olympic medal; some came back to compete in the next Olympics.

3. Draw a map of the different areas of unrest during the Carter-Reagan administrations.

4. Write a report on the Ayatollah Khomeini and his hostages. How do released hostages cope with their freedom after their ordeal is over?

5. Write a short biography on Geraldine Ferraro, the first woman vice-presidential candidate of a major political party.

GEORGE H. W. BUSH
(1924–   , P. 1989–1993)

George Herbert Walker Bush had often taken the hard way in his life, which helped him face the difficulties of building an alliance against Saddam Hussein and Iraq in 1991. Success in that war led to one of the highest approval ratings in history for a president, 89 percent, yet he lost the election only a year later.

Bush was born into the very wealthy family of Prescott Bush in 1924. As a boy, George attended Phillips Academy. Anxious to volunteer during World War II, he lied about his age to get into the Navy aviation program, and he became a pilot at 18. From 1942 to 1945, he flew 58 missions in the Pacific. During one mission he was shot down. For heroism, he was awarded the Distinguished Flying Cross. In 1945, he married Barbara Pierce, the daughter of a magazine publisher.

After the war, he attended Yale University where he captained the baseball team. Bush graduated with high grades. Instead of going into his father's investment business, the Bushes moved to Texas where he started his own oil company. In 1980, his reported wealth was $1.4 million. Bush lost a race for the Senate in 1964, but he won a House seat in 1966 and 1968. In 1970, he lost in his second try for a Senate seat. President Nixon appointed him United Nations ambassador from 1971 to 1972. In 1973–1974, he was chairman of the Republican National Committee; in 1974–1975, he was chief liaison officer in Peking; and he was director of the CIA in 1976–1977. In 1981, he became Ronald Reagan's vice president.

The election of 1988. In 1988, Reagan's popularity was very high, and that helped Bush win the nomination. For vice president, he chose a conservative, Senator Dan Quayle, from Indiana. The Democrats chose Governor Michael Dukakis of Massachusetts as their candidate. During the campaign, Bush assured the voters: "Read my lips—no new taxes." The Dukakis campaign stumbled from the beginning, and Bush easily defeated him 426–112 in electoral votes.

BUSH AS PRESIDENT. In his inaugural address, Bush said: "A new breeze is blowing, and the old bipartisanship must be made new again." However, Bush began his term with a slow start. With Democrats controlling both Houses of Congress, his appointments to the cabinet were carefully studied. Among his cabinet members were James Baker, secretary of state; Dick Cheney, secretary of defense; and Elizabeth Dole, secretary of labor.

In 1989, with revenues dropping because of a slowing economy and high deficits, Bush reluctantly agreed to a tax hike, breaking his "Read my lips" promise.

The recession in 1991 resulted from a drop in profits and less buying by consumers. Businesses began laying off workers, and unemployment jumped from 5.5 percent in 1990 to 6.5 percent in 1991 to 7.4 percent in 1992.

Some major issues occurred during Bush's presidency. One was the large oil spill from the tanker, *Exxon Valdez,* which occurred off the coast of Alaska. Another, the federal government had to rescue some savings and loans that had made unwise loans and whose presidents were paid very high salaries. Problems with drug trafficking and abuse also continued to cause great concern for state and federal officials.

Foreign affairs. Major changes in the world had a major effect on the United States and its foreign affairs. Since the Truman era, the Soviet Union and United States had engaged in the Cold War. The Soviets had the larger army, but the United States had a much larger navy and more advanced technology. By the time Bush came into office, the Soviets were falling behind, and their economy was in a state of confusion.

Other trouble spots, however, were becoming serious threats. The global economy is so complex that an epidemic in Africa led to a world-wide AIDS crisis, a drop in the Japanese and Singapore stock markets led to a drop in the U.S. stock markets, and war in the Middle East drew in nations dependent on oil. The international drug traffic threatened the United States. In 1988, a U.S. grand jury indicted General Noriega of Panama for drug trafficking. The next year, 24,000 U.S. troops were involved in an attempt to capture Noriega. He surrendered himself in January, and was convicted in Miami of drug trafficking.

The United States found itself involved in different parts of the world and facing new enemies. In 1991, two major events occurred: the Gulf War and the collapse of the Soviet Union.

The Gulf War. From 1980 to 1988, Iraq and its neighbor, Iran, fought a war that killed thousands on both sides. After the war, the ruler of Iraq, Saddam Hussein, found his nation in deep financial trouble. He wanted an easy victory to restore his reputation as a great leader in the Muslim world. In 1990, he threatened, then seized, the small, oil-rich neighbor country Kuwait. To frighten Saudi Arabia, he moved troops to the Arabian border. Other countries in the region gave their support to the Saudis, and the United States quickly sent a fleet, troops, and arms to support the Saudis.

Israel was also in danger of attack by Iraqi Scud missiles, so the United States sent Patriot missiles to Israel and Saudi Arabia to shoot down the Scuds. The United Nations condemned Iraq, and many nations sent troops to form a 600,000-man coalition army and air force surrounding Iraq.

Hussein rejected all demands that he pull out of Kuwait. On January 10, 1991, Congress authorized the use of force against Iraq; war began a week later with air attacks. Operation "Desert Storm" had begun. Iraq's capital, Baghdad, was hit with missiles and bombs that destroyed most of its communications operations. Iraq's Scud missiles were fired at Israel and Saudi Arabia, but most were destroyed by Patriot missiles.

In his State of the Union Address, Bush said the purpose of the war was to free Kuwait, not destroy Iraq. He warned that Iraq would be invaded unless it pulled out of Kuwait. Land fighting began on February 24, with 200,000 troops taking part in the attack. Some coalition troops moved into Kuwait, still others into Iraq. Retreating Iraqi forces set fire to many oil facilities before leaving Kuwait. They then began dumping oil into the Persian Gulf, creating an oil slick 60 miles long and 20 miles wide. On February 27, Bush announced that Kuwait was freed and Iraq's army defeated. The land war had lasted 100 hours, but Iraqi losses had been devastating: up to 100,000 killed and wounded, 175,000 captured, and about 3,700 tanks destroyed. The United States had 148 fatalities.

Hussein was still in power, however, and he defied the rules set down by the United Nations for inspection of his atomic and bacteriological warfare plants. Many Americans were convinced that the war should have continued until Hussein was forced out of office.

The breakup of the Soviet Union. Conditions in the Soviet Union worsened every day. While crops rotted in fields because transportation had broken down, food stores in cities had bare shelves. Workers complained that they were not being paid, and strikes were held. Oil could not be exported because the pipelines were old and leaking. The meltdown at Chernobyl indicated that shoddy construction in Russia was not only in its buildings but in its nuclear power plants as well. While the Communist Party leaders enjoyed great privileges, they did not make the changes that were needed for the rest of the nation.

Along with other members, Boris Yeltsin, leader of Russia's Soviet Socialist Republic, left the Communist party. In July 1991, Yeltsin defeated a Communist for the presidency of the Russian S.S.R. That August, eight Communist leaders attempted to seize control of the Soviet Union by arresting Mikhail Gorbachev; Yeltsin called for a general strike, and the eight leaders were arrested. Gorbachev and the Soviet Parliament suspended all Communist Party activities. This led to a breakup of the Soviet Union. The republics that had made up the U.S.S.R. were given the choice of leaving and forming independent nations or remaining in a new Commonwealth of Independent States. Estonia, Latvia, and Lithuania left, and President Bush recognized them in December 1991.

The election of 1992. The possibility of reducing military expenses, paying off some of the national debt, or putting money into social programs appealed to many in Congress but not to Bush. With rising unemployment, his popularity began to wane.

The Democrats chose Governor William (Bill) Clinton of Arkansas as their candidate. Bush easily won the Republican nomination. A third challenger, Texas billionaire Ross Perot, founded the Reform Party in an effort to reform American politics.

Clinton won by 5.8 million popular votes and 370–168 electoral votes over Bush. For the first time in 12 years, a Democrat was to occupy the White House. The Bushes retired to a new home in Houston, Texas. Later, Bush took pride in two sons becoming governors, George W. Bush in Texas and Jeb Bush in Florida. George W. Bush would then go on to be our 43rd president.

WILLIAM (BILL) CLINTON
(1946–   , P. 1993–2001)

While attending a Rose Garden ceremony honoring Boys State delegates, a teenager shook hands with President Kennedy. That occasion caused the young man to devote his life to public service. In 1993, William Jefferson Clinton took the oath of office and became the youngest president since Kennedy. His presidency was to be successful in some ways, but unfortunately marred by accusations of misconduct.

Clinton was born in Hope, Arkansas, in 1946. His father had been killed in a traffic accident three months before he was born. His mother was remarried when he was four years old to Roger Clinton. While he was in high school, Bill adopted his stepfather's last name. Two events of his high school years were important to him. He played saxophone in the band, (which he frequently played to entertain crowds during his political career); the other was his Boys State visit to the White House, which resulted in his resolution to go into politics.

Clinton received his bachelor's degree in foreign service from Georgetown University in 1968. He then attended Oxford University as a Rhodes Scholar for two years. Returning to the United States, he attended Yale University where he met Hillary Rodham, a fellow student. He received his law degree from Yale in 1973 and returned to Arkansas where he taught law at the University of Arkansas while preparing to enter politics.

In 1974, Clinton lost his race for Congress from the Arkansas Third District. The next year, he married Hillary Rodham. In 1976, he was elected as the Arkansas attorney general, and he became governor in 1978. He lost his re-election bid four years later, but then regained the office in 1986 and was governor from then until 1992.

The election of 1992. George H.W. Bush was again the presidential nominee of the Republicans. After defeating other rivals for the Democratic nomination, Clinton focused on the economy, which was not doing well. The third candidate in the campaign was Ross Perot, a billionaire who attracted much attention with his criticisms of governmental inefficiency. Bush believed government was too big and spent too much. Clinton argued that government had a major part to play in putting America to work again.

Whether it was to save campaign money or to humanize the candidates, talk shows became a place for candidates to go to reach the public with their message.

Personal attacks on Clinton's character were sometimes bitter. He had avoided the draft and opposed the Vietnam War, and there were charges of infidelity and profiting from a failed Whitewater land scheme in Arkansas. Most Democratic attacks were on Vice President Dan Quayle whose blunders were commonly joked about on late-night television shows.

Clinton won the election by 370–168 in electoral votes and by 5.8 million popular votes. Perot came in third with 19.7 million popular votes.

CLINTON AS PRESIDENT (first term). Like many presidents before him, Clinton struggled in his first months in office. His first problem came in an argument with military leaders over allowing homosexuals to serve in the armed forces. They reached a compromise of: "Don't ask, don't tell." His budget was in trouble because of conservative demands that spending be cut and taxes lowered. Heated debates occurred over such issues as health care and welfare reform. Many of his proposals failed or were compromised, but he did win a victory in getting the North American Free Trade Agreement (NAFTA) passed. This made trade with Mexico and Canada easier. Congress eventually approved a budget deficit bill to slow the growth of the national debt; a bill to establish a waiting period before a person could buy handguns (the Brady Bill); and AmeriCorps, a national service program.

The Republicans, led by Newt Gingrich, gained control of the House and Senate in 1994. Republican conservatives put great effort into investigating charges made earlier about the Whitewater land deal and possible Clinton involvement. An independent counsel, Kenneth Starr, was appointed to investigate. His investigations spread to include many other matters, including the firing of workers at the White House travel office, the death of a White House lawyer, and cover-ups of Clinton infidelities.

Foreign and domestic issues continued to arise. Israel and Jordan signed a peace agreement in 1994 at the White House. Clinton tried to end "ethnic cleansing" in Bosnia without using U.S. troops, but by 1995, the United States joined other countries in sending "peace-keeping" troops to Bosnia. The president had difficulty in supporting Yeltsin against Communist critics in Russia while criticizing the Russian invasion of Chechnya, a region trying to break away from Russian domination.

The election of 1996. The Republicans chose Senator Bob Dole as their candidate to oppose Clinton in 1996. Ross Perot again entered the contest but with much less support than in 1992. To the average voter, the successful economy overshadowed the charges brought out in Starr's investigations. Clinton won over Dole by 379–159 in electoral votes and by 8.2 million popular votes. Perot had 11 million fewer votes than in 1992.

CLINTON AS PRESIDENT (second term). The issue dominating the next three years of the Clinton administration was that of the Paula Jones lawsuit and the Monica Lewinsky affair. Ms. Jones had charged that while he was governor of Arkansas, Clinton had made unwanted advances toward her. She then had sued him for sexual harassment. The case had been tied up in court for years, with Clinton publicly denying it had ever happened. Starr believed that it was true, however, and he was looking for information from other women. An intern at the White House, Monica Lewinsky, told a friend that she had had an affair with the president.

Clinton testified in a televised appearance before the Starr grand jury looking into charges of perjury in the Paula Jones case. Starr then took his charges of a cover-up to Congress. The House judiciary committee investigated and brought four charges of impeachment against Clinton. Public opinion polls indicated that most Americans believed the charges were politically motivated. In a tense House vote, two charges were dropped, but two impeachment charges passed. The Senate trial began on January 7, 1999, and was presided over by Chief Justice Rehnquist. The trial was shortened by the decision not to call witnesses. It ended with a not guilty vote of 45–55 on one charge, and 50–50 on the other, far short of the two-thirds required by the Constitution to remove a president from office.

While this issue was being settled, Clinton and other leaders were working on other problems as well. The Food and Drug Administration was attacking the sale of tobacco products to young people, and lawsuits by state attorneys general forced the tobacco companies to stop advertising on billboards and television. Internet, movie, and television producers were criticized for making violent and other objectionable materials available to young people.

A strong economy made it possible to create 22 million jobs, and unemployment dropped to four percent in June of 2000. With welfare rolls cut and restraint in federal spending, the federal government and most states were bringing in more taxes than ever before. At the same time, higher interest rates kept inflation under control. The stock market was higher than ever as well. With record amounts of tax money coming in, it was possible to begin paying off part of the national debt. In July 2000, the Treasury Department announced that $221 billion would be paid on the national debt that year. It was expected that there would be a $211 billion surplus for 2000. However, a threat to the nation's economy came from rising oil prices. These were caused by OPEC nations reducing oil production and the increased popularity of fuel-wasting vehicles.

World Affairs. The United States was much involved in world affairs during the Clinton administration. In some cases the United States was directly involved, while in others its prestige helped bring opposing sides to the bargaining table. Terrorism was taking on new forms, and nations had to work together to capture criminals. Drug dealers often crossed borders, and the United States worked with other nations to prevent drugs from entering the country.

The United States feared that nations like Iraq and Libya would receive missiles and other arms from the nations of the old Soviet Union. The United States and Russia agreed to destroy many missiles.

The Clinton administration also worked to bring warring peoples together. In Northern Ireland, the United States helped bring peace between warring Catholics and Protestants. The United States was also involved in talks between North and South Korea. The most difficult area was still the Middle East, where the United States, led by Secretary of State Madeleine Albright and other negotiators, continued to work with Israel, the Palestinians, and other Muslim neighbors to work out an agreement.

Many issues remained to be settled when the Clinton administration ended. These were topics for debate in the 2000 election, and the two candidates often proposed widely different ways of solving them.

Name: _____ Date: _____

Points to Ponder (G.H.W. Bush, Clinton)

1. What was Bush's background in foreign affairs?

   _____

   _____

   _____

2. What was the effect of Bush's statement: "Read my lips—no new taxes"?

   _____

   _____

   _____

   _____

3. Why was General Noriega brought to the United States? What happened to him?

   _____

   _____

   _____

   _____

4. What brought on "Desert Storm"? How did it end?

   _____

   _____

   _____

   _____

5. What caused the Cold War to end?

   _____

   _____

   _____

   _____

6. What were the major differences between Bush and Clinton on the role of government?

   _____

   _____

   _____

Name: _____ Date: _____

Points to Ponder (G.H.W. Bush, Clinton)

7. What happened in the impeachment of Clinton?

_____
_____
_____
_____

8. What nations were involved in creating NAFTA? What was its purpose?

_____
_____
_____

9. What was the effect of economic growth on the national debt?

_____
_____
_____

10. What were two types of problems requiring international cooperation?

_____
_____
_____

☆ ☆ ☆ **Explore History** ☆ ☆ ☆

1. George H.W. Bush received a Distinguished Flying Cross for heroism during World War II. Draw a picture of this. Research to find other people who have been awarded this honor. How does the government decide who receives the Distinguished Flying Cross?

2. Draw or cut out pictures and make a poster about the oil spill of the *Exxon Valdez* and its effect on wildlife, both on land and in the ocean.

3. Draw a map of the Soviet Union. Compare the Soviet Union before and after its breakup.

4. Try to find some cigarette ads from the past that promoted smoking. How has the public's awareness of smoking changed? What was the Food and Drug Administration's involvement? How did all this affect the tobacco companies?

5. Write a short report on the Brady Bill or AmeriCorps.

GEORGE W. BUSH

(1946–   , P. 2001–2009)

In January 2001, for the first time since John Quincy Adams became president, the son of a former president took the oath of office. Unlike his father, George H.W. Bush, George W. Bush was raised in Texas and was more content on his Texas ranch than in New England.

Bush was born in 1946, and he grew up in Midland and Houston, Texas. His mother ran the family because his father was often away on political or business trips. At the age of 15, he attended Phillips Academy prep school in Andover, Massachusetts. After receiving his bachelor's degree from Yale University, he became a pilot in the Texas Air National Guard. He later earned an MBA degree from Harvard and entered the oil business in Midland, Texas.

In 1977, George W. married Laura Welch, a school librarian, and found the focus he needed in his life. Her enthusiasm for education and books, along with the birth of their twin daughters in 1981, contributed to his interest in education.

Coming from a political family, it was natural for him to run for office. After losing his campaign for the U.S. House of Representatives seat in 1978, he returned to the oil business. At that time, he recognized that he had a drinking problem and was able to beat it with his strong faith and determination.

After working in his father's presidential campaign in 1988, Bush became managing partner for the Texas Rangers baseball team. He left the job when he was elected governor of Texas in 1994 in a close election. His main concern was improving public schools through better funding and student achievement tests. Districts were given more local control, and parents were given more choice in the schools their children attended. He also cut taxes and encouraged more business investment and job growth. In 1998, he won a second term as governor by a landslide. In that same year, his brother Jeb was elected governor of Florida.

The election of 2000. Winning the Republican nomination for president in 2000, he chose Dick Cheney as his running mate. Bush described himself as a compassionate conservative and wanted limited government, personal responsibility, strong families, and local control. He felt the best way to improve the economy was by cutting taxes. Cheney was popular with conservative Republicans and had wide experience in the oil business and in government, having served as a Congressman from Wyoming and in the Ford and the senior Bush administrations.

The Democratic candidate, Al Gore, was the son of a senator, had served in the U.S. Senate, and was the current vice president for President Clinton. The election was very close, and it was finally decided by the controversy over Florida's electoral votes. The results were not final until December when the U.S. Supreme Court ruled against any further recounts in Florida by a 5–4 vote. This gave Florida's electoral votes to Bush. The Republicans had also won control of the House in the election, and the Senate was evenly divided, with Vice President Cheney casting a vote in the case of a tie.

BUSH AS PRESIDENT (first term). In spite of the opposition of many Democrats, Bush pushed forward a number of his agenda items in domestic and foreign policy. Between 2001 and 2003 Bush was able to get Congress to pass tax cuts for all tax rates and increased the child tax credit. Critics charged that the cuts would benefit the rich more than the poor and would lead to budget deficits and cuts in social programs. Bush also supported free trade agreements with nations around the world.

Another proposal was to improve education with the No Child Left Behind Act signed into law on January 8, 2002. The program required states to set standards in reading and math skills for students. Testing would hold schools accountable for students meeting these standards. Those districts that failed would lose part of their federal funding.

Spending cuts were made in Amtrak, Medicaid, and social programs. Military spending was increased to make up for the deep cuts during the Clinton administration.

September 11, 2001. While domestic issues never die completely in importance, foreign problems sometimes upstage them. That happened after September 11, 2001, when a horrendous attack on the United States of America was conducted by an extremist Islamic group. The attacks were conducted against innocent American citizens, against the financial infrastructure of America, and the American military infrastructure. It began when the terrorists hijacked four airliners. Two of the planes were crashed into the World Trade Center towers in New York City, and a third plane was crashed into the Pentagon in Washington, D.C. The fourth hijacked airliner crashed into a field in Pennsylvania. Due to the heroic efforts of passengers on this last airliner, it did not make it to the intended destination, the White House. Some 3,000 people were killed by the attack. Congress quickly approved $54 billion to help the cities and states affected; millions were donated by Americans to help the victims' families.

The War on Terror. Those involved in the attack were terrorists linked to Osama bin Laden's Al Qaeda organization. Bin Laden was traced to Afghanistan where the Muslim radicals, the Taliban, ruled and protected him. The Taliban had made many enemies because of their cruel brutalities and harsh restrictions, so it was not hard for the United States to organize opposition to overthrow them. An international coalition of military forces invaded Afghanistan on October 7, 2001, with aerial bombings and eventually ground troops. The Taliban government was removed from power and Al Qaeda was driven into the mountains. While many of the Al Qaeda leaders were killed or captured, bin Laden remains at large.

Another Middle Eastern troublemaker was Saddam Hussein, the dictator of Iraq. He had long given the Sunni Muslims in Iraq preference over Iraqi Shi'ites and Kurds. After the first Iraq war, Hussein maintained control, but he was under the watchful eyes of the United States and the United Nations. His cruelty to his own people had long angered Americans. President Bush charged that Hussein had sent financial help to Al Qaeda and was storing weapons of mass destruction. In March 2003, the United States, Great Britain, and a coalition of 43 other countries launched an air and ground attack on Iraq that was highly successful. Hussein was eventually captured in December 2003. He was tried by an Iraqi special tribunal and executed December 30, 2006.

The Iraq war was unpopular in the Muslim world, and radicals went to Iraq to join the insurgents there in guerilla warfare against the United States, its allies, and those Iraqis who were for a new government. While the United States was eager to pull its troops out of Afghanistan and Iraq, it was necessary to help set up new governments in those countries. In both countries, free elections were held, despite terrorist threats. In both countries, the voter turnout was large, and interim governments were set up.

In the United States, the possibility of more terrorism led to forming the cabinet-level Department of Homeland Security. Security was tightened at airports and on aircraft, as well as at other parts of the country's infrastructure, such as power plants, railroads, and water treatment facilities. Many people believed the United States should have more protection on its borders and clamp down on illegal immigration.

The election of 2004. In 2004, George W. Bush was reelected with a 53 percent popular majority, defeating the Democratic Senator John Kerry and his running mate Senator John Edwards. Bush received the largest number of votes of any candidate in U.S. history. The northeast and west coasts voted heavily for Kerry, while Bush carried most other states.

BUSH AS PRESIDENT (second term). The Republicans dominated both houses of Congress, and Bush began pushing hard for some of the programs he had advocated in the campaign. He wanted to privatize Social Security, giving workers the choice of paying into the program or investing part of their money in private funds. This would allow their money to grow at a faster rate. Critics charged his proposal would be too costly and deprive Social Security of money it needs to pay bills. Other proposed cuts in social programs like Medicaid, transportation, and farm subsidies had some opposition in Congress. Over the Bush presidency, the U.S. national debt grew due to the added expense of fighting terrorism and the wars in Iraq and Afghanistan. Expanding some government programs also led to increased debt.

To ease the nation's dependency on foreign oil, Bush's proposal to drill for oil in Alaska passed, despite environmental concerns.

In 2007, President Bush was confronted with a new challenge. The price of homes had peaked in 2006 and begun to fall. Many people had taken out huge loans to buy real estate, convinced that the value would only go up. Financial institutions had heavily invested in this kind of debt because it was considered 'safe' debt. However, the widespread practice of lending people more than they could afford to pay back triggered a finacial collapse. The $150 billion Economic Stimulus Act passed in January 2008 provided tax refunds for lower- and middle-class families. It also provided more funding for government-backed mortgage lenders Fannie Mae and Freddie Mac to try to help homeowners threatened by foreclosure. However, banks froze credit in an attempt to survive, and several large banks, namely Bear Stearns and Lehman's, failed, which further paralyzed the system. President Bush and Congress then passed the Emergency Economic Stabilization Act on October 3, 2008. It authorized spending up to $700 billion to prop up the remaining banks. As President Bush left office in January 2009, the nation was in the middle of the most severe economic recession since the Great Depression.

☆ ☆ ☆ **Explore History**

1. George W. Bush's vice president, Dick Cheney, was the secretary of defense under former President George Bush and played a major part in Operation Desert Storm. Write a mini-report comparing Operation Desert Storm to the second invasion of Iraq known as Operation Iraqi Freedom.

2. Condoleezza Rice was an important member of the Bush administration. During George W. Bush's first term, Rice was the National Security Advisor. During Bush's second term, she was appointed secretary of state when Colin Powell stepped down. Research Condoleezza Rice's life and write a short biography.

Name: _____ Date: _____

Points to Ponder (G. W. Bush)

1. What did the election of George W. Bush have in common with that of John Quincy Adams?

    _____

2. What contributed to George W.'s interest in education?

    _____

    _____

3. Who did Bush choose for his vice presidential running mate in the campaign of 2000? Why did he choose him?

    _____

    _____

    _____

4. What was unique about the election of 2000?

    _____

    _____

    _____

    _____

5. What did Bush do to help tax-paying families and individuals?

    _____

    _____

6. Who was behind the terrorist attack on September 11, 2001?

    _____

7. With what country did the United States go to war to stop the extremist Islamic group?

    _____

8. Who was captured in December 2003?

    _____

    _____

9. What cabinet-level department was created after September 11, 2001?

    _____

10. The economic crisis of 2008 was brought about by a failure of what type of lending?

    _____

BARACK H. OBAMA
(1961–   , P. 2009–   )

Barack Obama was born in Honolulu, Hawaii, on August 4, 1961, to a white mother from Kansas and a black father from Kenya. His parents divorced when he was four, and his mother married an Indonesian student. From 1967 to 1971, Obama lived with his family in Indonesia. In 1971, he returned to Hawaii and lived with his maternal grandparents until he went to college.

Obama graduated from Columbia University in 1983 and worked as a community organizer on Chicago's South Side before going to Harvard Law School in 1988. There, he was elected the first black president of the Harvard Law Review. After graduation, he was a professor of constitutional law at the Universtiy of Chicago Law School. He met Michelle Robinson in 1989, and they married in 1991. They have two daughters, Malia and Sasha.

In 1996, Obama was elected to the Illinois state senate. He served there until 2004. After an unsuccessful run for a seat in the U.S. House of Representatives in 2000, he ran for U.S. Senate in 2004. Obama's keynote address at the 2004 Democratic National Convention in July, helped bring him to the attention of the nation. He easily won the senate seat in November, becoming the fifth African-American senator in history and only the third to be popularly elected. He soon began to be talked about as a future contender for the office of president.

The election of 2008. The Democratic candidates campaigned hard on withdrawing troops from Iraq and establishing a functioning government in Afghanistan. Early in the campaign, Hillary Clinton, wife of former president Bill Clinton, was considered the Democratic frontrunner. However, the young senator from Illnios, Barack Obama, unified the party with a message of hope and change, and after the long primary season, he was chosen as the Democratic candidate. Joe Biden, a long-time senator from Delaware, was chosen as the Democratic vice presidential candidate.

The Republicans endorsed Senator John McCain as their candidate. He was a decorated Vietnam veteran and prisoner of war and a popular, experienced senator from Arizona. He chose Sarah Palin, the governor of Alaska, as his running mate. This was only the second time a major party had nominated a female vice presidential candidate.

Then the economy froze up in the worst recession since the Great Depression. Both candidates returned to Washington, D.C., for votes on financial relief measures, and they developed plans to salvage the economy. McCain favored a continued military presence in Iraq, while Obama wanted to end military involvement there. Obama also focused on increasing America's energy independence and providing universal health care.

On Election Day, voters elected Barack Obama president. He won 52.9% of the popular vote and got 365 electoral votes to McCain's 173.

OBAMA AS PRESIDENT. Obama was the first African-American elected president, and the fourth-youngest man elected to the job. He took the oath of office on January 20, 2009. Obama chose his former oponent in the Democratic primary campaign, Hillary Clinton, to head the State Department.

President Obama began work by issuing executive orders directing the U.S. military to draw up plans for withdrawing troops from Iraq. He also ordered the closing of the detention camp at Guantanamo Bay in Cuba that housed suspected terrorists. Some of those prisoners would be sent to facilities in Iraq and Afghanistan. Others would be housed at a maximum-security prison in Thomson, Illinois, despite great opposition to bringing the terror suspects to American soil.

The first bill President Obama signed into law was the Lilly Ledbetter Fair Pay Act on January 29, 2009. This made it easier for workers to file employment discrimination lawsuits. He also signed legislation reauthorizing a program to provide insurance for uninsured children. In March, he lifted the ban on federal tax dollars being used to fund embryonic stem cell research.

Early in his term, Obama got the opportunity to make a lasting impression on the judicial branch of government. He appointed Sonia Sotomayor as an associate justice of the Supreme Court to replace the retiring David Souter. Sotomayor was confirmed by the Senate on August 6, 2009. She is the first Hispanic and the third woman to be a Supreme Court justice.

The Obama administration's domestic policy has been focused on dealing with the economic crisis and pushing for legislation to reform the health care system. President Obama signed the American Recovery and Reinvestment Act on February 17, 2009. This provided $787 billion to help the economy recover from the worldwide recession by spending money on health care, infrastructure, education, tax breaks and incentives, and direct assistance to individuals over the course of several years. The federal government also put billions of taxpayer dollars into the automotive industry in a takeover of Chrysler and General Motors as those companies went through bankruptcy.

Heated debate over the reform of health care began in July 2009 and was the major focus of Congress in the fall. Despite opposition from voters in public meetings held throughout the summer and little support from Republicans, the House and Senate passed separate versions of the health care reform bill by December 24, 2009. However, public support for the bill dropped as people and Congress turned their attention to the economy. The Republicans were also able to win the senate seat from Massachusetts, so the Democrats no longer had the 60-vote supermajority needed to pass a bill without debate. A final compromise health care reform bill was yet to be worked out at the time of this printing.

In foreign policy, President Obama announced that combat operations in Iraq would end by August 31, 2010. However, smaller numbers of U.S. military forces would still be in Iraq for some time to support the Iraqi military and police as they take over the work of stopping insurgent attacks and terrorists. Throughout 2009, insurgent attacks against U.S. and coalition military personnel increased in Afghanistan as the Taliban regained strength. Soldiers were already being shifted from Iraq to Afghanistan, but in the summer of 2009, the U.S. military commander Lt. General Stanley McChrystal asked for up to 40,000 more troops. President Obama announced in December 2009 that 30,000 troops would be sent to Afghanistan over the next year, but that U.S. military involvement would begin to be reduced by July 2011.

In an unexpected honor, the Norwegian Nobel Committee awarded the 2009 Nobel Peace Prize to President Obama for "his extraordinary efforts to strengthen international diplomacy and cooperation between peoples." Many of his critics said he had not accomplished enough to deserve the award. However, Obama accepted the award as a call to action to promote peace even as the United States was fighting two wars and sending more troops to Afghanistan.

After one year in office, President Obama's approval rating had dropped to below 50% with many people declining in their support of his policies, worried about the unemployment rate barely under 10%, and becoming frustrated that more had not been accomplished.

Name: _____ Date: _____

Points to Ponder (Obama)

1. Where was Barack Obama born?

    _____

2. What first brought Barack Obama to the nation's attention?

    _____

    _____

3. To what office was Obama elected in 2004? What was noteworthy about this?

    _____

    _____

4. Who were the Democratic and Republican candidates for president and vice president in 2008?

    _____

    _____

5. What was the first bill that President Obama signed into law?

    _____

6. Who was being held at the detention camp at Guantanamo Bay in Cuba?

    _____

7. On what was the money in the American Recovery and Reinvestment Act to be spent?

    _____

    _____

8. Debate on what kind of bill took up most of the last half of 2009 in the House of Respresentatives and the Senate?

    _____

9. While troops were being withdrawn from Iraq, where were more troops being sent?

    _____

10. What honor was awarded to President Obama in 2009?

    _____

 **Explore History**

In order to become less involved in the Middle East, it is recommended that America become less dependent on foreign oil. List some of the ways Americans could use less foreign oil. What are some alternative fuels being developed?

Name: _____ Date: _____

Quiz: Who Was President?

Who was president when each of these events occurred? Since some of the presidents had the same last name, use J. Adams for John Adams, J.Q. Adams for John Quincy Adams, W.H. Harrison for William Henry Harrison, B. Harrison for Benjamin Harrison, A. Johnson for Andrew Johnson, L. Johnson for Lyndon Johnson, T. Roosevelt for Theodore Roosevelt, F. Roosevelt for Franklin Roosevelt, G.H.W. Bush for George Herbet Walker Bush, and G.W. Bush for George Walker Bush.

_____ 1. 1813 - Oliver Perry won battle on Lake Erie

_____ 2. 1798 - Sedition Act is passed

_____ 3. 1795 - Jay Treaty approved by Senate

_____ 4. 1807 - *Chesapeake* Affair

_____ 5. 1800 - Presidents begin living in White House

_____ 6. 1789 - Bill of Rights added to Constitution

_____ 7. 1802 - U.S. Military Academy opens

_____ 8. 1811 - Battle of Tippecanoe

_____ 9. 1821 - Santa Fe trade opens

_____ 10. 1803 - The case of *Marbury v. Madison* is decided

_____ 11. 1814 - "Star-Spangled Banner" is written

_____ 12. 1825 - Erie Canal opens

_____ 13. 1819 - Spain surrenders Florida to United States

_____ 14. 1828 - Construction begins on B & O, America's first railroad

_____ 15. 1836 - Battle of the Alamo

_____ 16. 1841 - "Old Tippecanoe" enters office

_____ 17. 1845 - Texas annexed just before end of his term

_____ 18. 1833 - A president rides a train for the first time

_____ 19. 1837 - Major financial panic occurs

_____ 20. 1848 - Gold discovered in California

_____ 21. 1851 - Commodore Matthew Perry sent to open trade with Japan

_____ 22. 1844 - First telegraph message is sent

_____ 23. 1849 (April) - Safety pin patented by Walter Hunt

Name: _____ Date: _____

Quiz: Who Was President? (cont.)

_____ 24. 1850 (September) - Compromise of 1850 passed

_____ 25. 1860 - Pony Express service opens

_____ 26. 1848 - Mexican War ends

_____ 27. 1865 - President is shot and killed

_____ 28. 1859 - John Brown attacks Harper's Ferry

_____ 29. 1863 - Battle of Gettysburg is fought

_____ 30. 1854 - Kansas-Nebraska Act is passed

_____ 31. 1861 (April) - Fort Sumter is fired upon

_____ 32. 1868 - Fourteenth Amendment is ratified

_____ 33. 1881 (September) - President dies from wounds

_____ 34. 1876 - Telephone is tested by Bell

_____ 35. 1867 - Alaska ceded to United States by Russia

_____ 36. 1879 - Light bulb invented by Edison

_____ 37. 1869 - President nearly removed by impeachment trial

_____ 38. 1883 - Chinese immigration restricted

_____ 39. 1881 (May) - American Red Cross organized

_____ 40. 1886 - Statue of Liberty is dedicated

_____ 41. 1883 - Standard time adopted

_____ 42. 1890 - Sherman Anti-Trust Act is passed

_____ 43. 1895 - Revolt breaks out in Hawaii

_____ 44. 1898 - Battleship _Maine_ is sunk in Havana

_____ 45. 1903 - Wright brothers' first flight

_____ 46. 1898 - Battle of Manila Bay

_____ 47. 1907 - U.S. battleships begin world tour

_____ 48. 1909 (April) - Peary reaches the North Pole

_____ 49. 1901 - President killed by a radical

_____ 50. 1914 - World War I breaks out in Europe

Name: _____ Date: _____

Quiz: Who Was President? (cont.)

_____ 51. 1913 (February) - Amendment gives power to tax incomes

_____ 52. 1922 - First woman chosen for U.S. Senate

_____ 53. 1920 - Amendment gives U.S. women right to vote

_____ 54. 1927 - Lindbergh flies from New York to Paris

_____ 55. 1918 - Fourteen Points outlined by president

_____ 56. 1922 - Tomb of the Unknown Soldier is dedicated

_____ 57. 1929 (May) - First motion picture "Oscars" awarded

_____ 58. 1931 - "Star-Spangled Banner" becomes national anthem

_____ 59. 1924 - Details of Teapot Dome Scandal revealed

_____ 60. 1910 - President throws first ball to open baseball season

_____ 61. 1922 - First demonstration of a helicopter

_____ 62. 1929 (October) - The stock market crash

_____ 63. 1916 - Jeanette Rankin elected first woman in U.S. House

_____ 64. 1932 - Army of unemployed veterans marches on Washington

_____ 65. 1933 (June) - FDIC created to protect bank deposits

_____ 66. 1960 - U-2 incident

_____ 67. 1950 - Korean War begins

_____ 68. 1933 (March 31) - CCC gives jobs to unemployed young men

_____ 69. 1941 - Pearl Harbor attacked

_____ 70. 1948 - Marshall Plan helps Europe back on its feet

_____ 71. 1956 - Russia launches *Sputnik* into space

_____ 72. 1945 (August) - Atomic bomb dropped on Hiroshima

_____ 73. 1962 - Cuban missile crisis

_____ 74. 1935 - Social Security created

_____ 75. 1954 - Supreme Court rules segregated schools are unconstitutional

_____ 76. 1944 - D-Day invasion of Europe

_____ 77. 1963 - President killed by Lee Harvey Oswald

Name: _____ Date: _____

Quiz: Who Was President? (cont.)

_____ 78. 2003 - Saddam Hussein captured by U.S. forces

_____ 79. 1949 - NATO created

_____ 80. 1961 (March 1) - Peace Corps created

_____ 81. 1964 - Civil Rights Act is passed

_____ 82. 1965 - Medicare passes to provide health care to older Americans

_____ 83. 1975 - South Vietnam surrenders

_____ 84. 1968 - Martin Luther King, Jr., assassinated

_____ 85. 1972 - Watergate break-in at Democratic headquarters

_____ 86. 1991 - Persian Gulf War

_____ 87. 1981 - New president gets major tax cuts

_____ 88. 1989 (November) - Berlin Wall falls

_____ 89. 2009 (October) - President wins Nobel Peace Prize

_____ 90. 1979 - Iranian hostage crisis begins

_____ 91. 1973 - Vice President Agnew resigns

_____ 92. 1990 - U.S. population reaches 250 million

_____ 93. 1974 - President pardons the previous president

_____ 94. 1983 - President proposes "Star Wars" technology

_____ 95. 2008 - Subprime mortgage failures lead to global financial crisis

_____ 96. 1995 - Terrorist attack on federal building in Oklahoma City

_____ 97. 1969 (June) - United States lands men on the moon

_____ 98. 2009 (January 22) - President orders Guantanamo Bay detention camp closed "as soon as practicable"

_____ 99. 2001 (September) - Terrorist attacks on World Trade Center towers and Pentagon

_____ 100. 1999 - President tried for impeachment in Senate on charges he lied to grand jury. He was found not guilty.

List of Presidential Firsts

Washington: Only president never to have lived in Washington, D.C.
                    First president to refuse a third term

Adams: First president to reside in Washington, D.C.
                    First president whose son also became president

Jefferson: First president sworn into office in Washington, D.C.
                    First president who had been a governor

Madison: First president who had served in Congress
                    First president to regularly wear trousers instead of knee breeches

Monroe: First president who had been a senator
                    First president inaugurated outdoors

J.Q. Adams: First president to wear long pants at his inauguration
                    First president elected by a minority of the voters

Jackson: First president chosen by a national nominating convention
                    First president to ride on a railroad train

Van Buren: First president born in New York

W.H. Harrison: First president to die in office
                    Only president whose grandson also became president

Tyler: First vice president to become president because of the president's death
                    First president whose wife died while he was in office

Polk: First president survived by his mother

Taylor: First president who had never served in Congress or the Continental
                    Congress

Fillmore: First president to have a stepmother

Pierce: First president whose vice president never served in office

Buchanan: First and only president who never married
                    First president born in Pennsylvania

Lincoln: First president born in Kentucky
                    First president assassinated

A. Johnson: First president impeached
                    First president whose background was not military or legal

Grant: First president whose parents were both alive when he was inaugurated

Hayes: First president to take the oath of office in the White House

Garfield: First left-handed president

Arthur: First president born in Vermont

Cleveland: First Democrat to be elected president after the Civil War
First president elected to non-consecutive terms

McKinley: First presidential inauguration recorded by a motion picture camera

T. Roosevelt: First president to receive the Nobel Peace Prize
Youngest president at the time he took office

Taft: Only president who later became a chief justice of the Supreme Court

Wilson: First president who had been president of a major university
Only president with an earned Ph.D. degree

Harding: First president to ride to his inauguration in an automobile

Coolidge: Only president sworn in by his father
First president sworn in by a former president (Taft)

Hoover: First president born in Iowa

F. Roosevelt: First defeated vice presidential nominee to be elected president

Truman: First president born in Missouri

Eisenhower: First president born in Texas
First president who had ever been a five-star general

Kennedy: First Roman Catholic president
Only president who won a Pulitzer Prize

L. Johnson: First president sworn in on an airplane
First president sworn in wearing a business suit

Nixon: First president to visit China
First president to resign

Ford: First president who had never been elected president or vice president
First president to pardon a former president (Nixon)

Carter: First president who had been a submarine captain

Reagan: First movie actor to be elected president

Bush: First navy aviator who later became president

Clinton: First president born in Arkansas
First Rhodes Scholar to become president

G.W. Bush: First president to have been involved in a case heard by the Supreme
Court regarding his election to the presidency
First president to have owned a baseball team

Obama: First African-American president
First president born in Hawaii

Answer Keys

Points to Ponder

Students may have opinions that are different from those of the teacher, other students, or those included in this section. If the student "marches to a different drummer," the teacher should consider accepting his or her answer as valid.

WASHINGTON (page 9)

1. Some of Washington's qualities might include: his strength, his adventures, his willingness to take risks, his appearance, and his social skills.
2. Possible answers: used to rugged life outdoors, trained as a soldier by his brother, learned responsibility, fought in battles, defended frontier with poorly-trained recruits, learned how to lose without giving up
3. Possible answers: his size and appearance, experience, dignity, willingness to listen to different ideas and approaches to problems
4. Some possible answers: his being a slave owner, our reluctance to accept anyone as a hero, bad reaction to legends about him (cherry tree and crossing the Delaware, for examples)
5. Some possible answers: his leadership ability, being decisive, organizing an army, and popular image; A general might expect everyone (including Congress) to obey, not being familiar with the way politicians work.

JOHN ADAMS (page 11)

1. He was smart and patriotic, but would have a problem getting elected today.
2. OPINION. YES. People often judge a president by appearance, and whether or not he looks like a leader. NO. It's not appearance, but policies that count.
3. A party split is very difficult for any president to overcome. He can count on the opposing party to fight him, and if his own party is split, he will find it very hard to get anything accomplished.
4. The answer will most likely be yes, but there might be a variety of thoughts on the subject.
5. Freedom of speech, press, and peaceable assembly

JEFFERSON (page 15)

1. His intelligence, his interest in many subjects, and his use of words
2. He was wealthy, busy with being a lawyer and a farmer, recently married.
3. It persuaded many people that Americans had a right to revolt. It proclaimed the right of every person to "life, liberty and the pursuit of happiness."

4. OPINION. YES. Situations change, and the president has to change with them. NO. People voted for him to do one thing, and he is going against his word.
5. The Supreme Court declared an act of Congress unconstitutional and began to play an important role for the first time.
6. Everything a person does or has done in public life is open to public discussion.

MADISON (page 19)

1. You might have thought him weak and sickly and a bookworm.
2. The House of Representatives, because the size of a state's delegation depends on population
3. Dolley was outgoing, made friends easily, and helped her husband develop social skills. *This might be an opportunity to discuss the role of a political candidate's spouse.*
4. War with England
5. Andrew Jackson and William Henry Harrison
6. The public turned against the Federalists and accused them of being traitors.

MONROE (page 23)

1. There was only one political party, and national pride was strong.
2. Battle of Trenton
3. Monroe served in the legislature and as governor.
4. No more fleets on the Great Lakes, and the boundary was settled from Lake of the Woods to the crest of the Rocky Mountains.
5. To chase the Indians who had been raiding in Georgia; Great Britain and Spain
   He was too popular and Secretary of State Adams had spoken up for him.
6. Europe was to stay out of the Americas; the United States would stay out of Europe's affairs.

J. Q. ADAMS (page 26)

1. He was educated in Dutch and French schools.
2. No. He was overseas most of the time in Holland, Prussia, Portugal, Sweden, Great Britain, and Russia. Except for five years in the Senate, he had very little experience in U.S. politics.
3. Probably not. Opponents were sure to jump on it and accuse him of making a corrupt deal to get the job.
4. Everything he tried to accomplish had been defeated for political reasons.
5. He might have added a wider view of the whole picture, rather than just a local view, as well as adding the prestige of having a former president as a member.

JACKSON (page 31)

1. He was struck across his face and hand by a British officer for refusing to clean his boots.
2. She was married to Captain Robards and Jackson at the same time. No, she thought Robards had already received a divorce.
   Mrs. Jackson died, and Jackson blamed her death on attacks by the opposition.
3. One of his men said he was as tough as hickory.
4. "The spoils system" means that the winner chooses friends for government jobs.
5. The federal government would lose the ability to make decisions. If a state nullified a law it didn't like, another state would nullify another law.

VAN BUREN (page 34)

1. It was a Democratic political organization in New York that gave out jobs and punished officeholders who did not follow the party line.
2. Van Buren saw that Jackson would win. Jackson made him secretary of state.
3. The Panic was caused by too much economic growth, speculation, and high interest rates. Van Buren was the most concerned with how it affected government deposits in banks.
4. Yes; Student opinions may vary on whether or not the president deserves the blame.
5. He opposed annexing a slave state. He had sided with slavery before.

W. H. HARRISON, TYLER (page 38)

1. Earlier Harrison had opposed slavery, but later he took the more popular view that slavery was legal and citizens should have the right to own slaves.
2. The Indians waited to shoot a man on a gray horse. His horse had broken its rope and wandered off, so Harrison used another horse instead.
3. Harrison became a Whig because he didn't like Andrew Jackson.
4. Harrison's inaugural address was the longest ever given, 105 minutes long and 8,578 words.
5. No, he disagreed with the Whigs on most issues.
6. There was no official announcement of his death by the government, which was the only time in U.S. history that happened.

POLK (page 41)

1. Jackson
2. Oregon
3. Yes; He was not even mentioned in the first seven ballots of the Democratic Convention.
4. Opponents said the United States was bullying a weak neighbor and that the war was an excuse to expand slavery.

5. OPINION. One argument might be that he accomplished a great deal in gaining new lands for the United States. Another argument might be that he took advantage of a weak neighbor and does not deserve to be called great.

TAYLOR, FILLMORE (page 45)

1. Old Rough and Ready; He dressed simply, ate simple food, and lived in a tent the same way his men did.
2. Free Soilers opposed expanding slavery into the territories. They chose Van Buren.
3. For the North: California admission and an end to the slave trade in the District of Columbia; For the South: a stronger fugitive slave law
4. Matthew Perry went. The agreement was to help shipwrecked sailors. It was important because it was the first treaty Japan had made with anyone for centuries.
5. He supported McClellan, the Democrat.

PIERCE, BUCHANAN (page 50)

1. The Whigs made fun of his record. They said he had fainted in two battles, gotten sick in a third, and had missed the fourth battle.
2. Pierce saw his son get run over by a railroad car.
3. His party blamed him for the troubles in Kansas and for not being successful as president.
4. He blamed anti-slavery agitators in the North. Among them were Harriet Beecher Stowe, Henry Ward Beecher, William Lloyd Garrison, and John Brown.
5. Southern states started seceding. By the time Lincoln came into office, seven had left.

LINCOLN (page 55)

1. He had very little education. His favorite book was the Bible.
2. He paid off $1,000 in debts after his store had closed.
3. Lincoln opposed the Mexican War.
4. Confederates opened fire, which started the Civil War.
5. Mobile Bay and Atlanta
6. On April 9, Lee surrendered at Appomattox Courthouse to Grant.
   On April 14, Lincoln was shot by John Wilkes Booth at Ford's Theater. Lincoln died the next day.

A. JOHNSON, GRANT, HAYES (pages 62–63)

1. Johnson refused to give up his seat and leave with his seceding state.
2. Tenure of Office Act; He came within one vote of being removed from office.
3. His Congressman had turned in Grant's name incorrectly to West Point. He liked it better because it made his initials U.S. Grant instead of H.U.G.

4. He was a failure, he'd been forced out of the army; he had failed as a farmer and had worked in his father's leather shop.
5. Grant listened to bad advice from friends and wealthy admirers.
6. The Ku Klux Klan scared off blacks who tried to vote.
7. Hayes had been major general and was wounded five times.
8. Blaine was accused of receiving bribes. Hayes had always been honest.

GARFIELD, ARTHUR, CLEVELAND (page 70)
1. William Henry Harrison, Zachary Taylor, and Abraham Lincoln.
2. Morality was low. People paid bribes and gave gifts to officials to get what they wanted. At elections, they supported the candidates who had done favors for them.
3. Arthur was more like Garfield. He pushed for civil service reform, and ignored Conkling.
4. He forced cattlemen and logging companies off government land.
5. It gave the federal government the power to regulate interstate railroads.

B. HARRISON, CLEVELAND (page 74)
1. Grandfather, war record, support for Garfield might be likely answers.
2. It made it easier to sell their goods against foreign competition.
3. It made the price of goods they purchased cheaper.
4. It caused a drop in steel and coal production, which caused layoffs. 2.5 million people were out of work.
5. Coxey wanted the unemployed to be hired to build roads. He was arrested for walking on the White House lawn.
6. OPINION. Probably not; HARRISON: He didn't have much personality, did not appeal to the public, and had poor personal relations. CLEVELAND: Probably not; He did not campaign, he was too one-sided in labor disputes, and was too interested in keeping the gold supply up while millions went hungry.

McKINLEY, T. ROOSEVELT (page 80)
1. The government should own them.
2. McKinley called out the National Guard to protect property, but raised money to keep strikers from starving.
3. McKinley stood on the front porch and gave short speeches. Bryan spoke around the country. Bryan was more like modern campaigners.

4. The Battleship *Maine* was sunk in Havana Harbor and people blamed it on the Spanish.
5. Roosevelt led the Rough Rider charge up San Juan Hill.
6. He established the merit system, fought graft, and fired those who were not doing their jobs.

TAFT, WILSON (pages 86–87)
1. Taft turned down the offer because the Filipinos begged him to stay.
2. Roosevelt went on an African safari.
3. Taft threw the first ball of the baseball season and started the "seventh-inning stretch."
4. Pinchot was a good friend of Roosevelt. His firing made Roosevelt think that Taft had been a bad choice for his successor.
5. Harding made him chief justice of the Supreme Court.
6. He had grown up in the South during and after the Civil War.
7. Wilson felt the other person should do the compromising.
8. The tariff was lowered and the Federal Reserve created.
9. Germany had to sign the treaty or be invaded.
10. The treaty and league were rejected by the Senate. [Other nations did accept it, and it became the League of Nations]. After World War II, the United Nations was created.

HARDING, COOLIDGE (page 92)
1. He liked the social life and mixing with other politicians. He usually sided with business.
2. They did their jobs well and were making improvements that caused people to believe things were going fine. Harding helped by not interfering.
3. He put friends into office who were out to make as much money as possible for themselves. Harding was not really prepared for the job.
4. He became famous because of the Boston Police Strike.
5. Coolidge cut government expenses.

HOOVER, F. ROOSEVELT (pages 100–101)
1. He was trained as an engineer and had become famous around the world for his success. The "great humanitarian" title came from his relief work in Belgium and Europe after World War I.
2. Hoover said prosperity was on his side.
3. He called meetings of business and government leaders to urge them to spend more, but business was afraid, and the states had little tax money coming in.

4. Wilson gave it to him because of his support in the 1912 election.
5. By the time FDR entered office, 5,500 banks had closed, 1 out of 4 workers were unemployed, and many farmers had lost their land.
6. FDR created AAA, which took land out of production and slaughtered pigs. You would not have liked it since you could hardly afford to buy food, even at lower prices.
7. Southern Democrats and Republicans joined to block programs.
8. The Four Freedoms Speech listed the four principles FDR considered essential for world peace: freedom of speech, freedom of religion, freedom from want, and freedom from fear. He made the speech to encourage Americans to support those who were fighting in WWII.
9. Japan attacked Pearl Harbor. The United States declared war on Japan on December 8 and on Germany and Italy on December 11.
10. He traveled to Casablanca, Cairo, and Yalta. He had trouble with Stalin, the leader of the Soviet Union.

TRUMAN, EISENHOWER (pages 108–109)
1. Truman lacked education, experience, and military background many thought he needed.
2. The Truman Committee was formed to fight waste and corruption in the building of military camps.
3. The OPA was dropped, and there were no controls on prices. With prices jumping, labor unions demanded higher wages.
4. The Marshall Plan was to build up European economies.
5. He had led invasions of Africa, Sicily, Italy, and Normandy.
6. The new line was near where it had been at the beginning of the war.
7. It said that segregation in education was unconstitutional.
8. A U.S. U-2 spy plane was shot down deep inside Russian territory.

KENNEDY, L. B. JOHNSON (pages 116–117)
1. His PT boat was sunk, and he towed a crew member to an island.
2. Kennedy sent 600 deputy U.S. marshals to restore order.
3. The invaders were captured. Khruschev tried to force the United States out of West Berlin. When that didn't work, he put up the Berlin Wall.
4. It became tense because no one was sure what might happen if the United States stopped a Russian ship. It ended when the Russian ships were ordered to return home.

5. Green Berets were sent to show the South Vietnamese army how to win.
6. He had served in the House and Senate and had been minority and majority leader in the Senate.
7. The Civil Rights Act made it illegal to discriminate in public places on the basis of race. It cut off federal programs to communities allowing discrimination.
8. The public did not like Goldwater's conservative views. He and his party were badly defeated in the election.
9. They disliked him and spoke of revolution and violence.
10. The goal was to convince North Vietnam they could not win, so the United States sent more troops. The public turned against the war and Johnson.

NIXON, FORD (pages 123–124)
1. He became famous for going after Alger Hiss, who was accused of having been a Communist.
2. Nixon had been accused of receiving $18,000 from wealthy men. He said that the only gift he had received was Checkers, his daughters' pet dog.
3. Nixon had lost the presidential race in 1960, then the governor's race in 1962.
4. Oil prices rose because of OPEC's cuts in production. It did not help him.
5. Agnew was forced to resign because of criminal charges. Ford was chosen to replace him (see Twenty-fifth Amendment to the Constitution).
6. Conversations about the Watergate cover-up could be heard to decide if the charge was true.
7. The Supreme Court ordered Nixon to turn the tapes over to the prosecutor.
8. Ford succeeded to the office when Nixon was impeached.
9. Ford said he did it to start the healing process after Watergate and to save Nixon and his family further suffering. The public did not like it.
10. Both governments lost to the Communists and surrendered.

CARTER, REAGAN (pages 130–131)
1. To always do your best and the importance of detailed planning.
2. He had begun the campaign with no money or name recognition and was open about being a born-again Christian.
3. The United States needed energy, but Three Mile Island's near-disaster discouraged building more nuclear power plants.
4. The United States opened diplomatic and trade relations with China. Russian relations were worse after Russian troops were sent into Afghanistan.
5. He was a radio sportscaster, movie actor, and television host.